# INVITATION TO LANGUAGES

## *Activities Workbook*
### *and*
## *Student Tape Manual*

Conrad J. Schmitt

**Glencoe
McGraw-Hill**

New York, New York    Columbus, Ohio    Woodland Hills, California    Peoria, Illinois

*Glencoe/McGraw-Hill*

*A Division of The McGraw·Hill Companies*

Copyright © 1998 by Glencoe/McGraw-Hill. All rights reserved. Except as permitted under the United States Copyright Act, no part of this publication may be reproduced or distributed in any form or by any means, or stored in a database or retrieval system, without the prior permission of the publisher.

Send all inquiries to:
**Glencoe/McGraw-Hill**
21600 Oxnard Street, Suite 500
Woodland Hills, CA 91367

ISBN 0-02-640867-8

Printed in the United States of America

4 5 6 7 8 9 066 03 02 01 00 99 98

# Table of Contents

# Welcome to *Spanish!*

# Saludos

**A** Select an appropriate response and circle the corresponding letter.

1. ¡Hola!
   a. ¡Hola!
   b. Gracias.
   c. Estupendo.

2. ¿Qué tal?
   a. Gracias.
   b. ¿Y tú?
   c. Muy bien.

3. Buenos días.
   a. Buenas noches.
   b. Estupendo.
   c. Buenos días.

**B** In the illustrations below, which people are probably saying *hola* and which are probably saying *buenos días?* Write A for those saying *hola* and B for those saying *buenos días.*

1. _____

2. _____

3. _____

4. _____

5. _____

**C** **Look at these clocks. Match each clock with the appropriate expression.**

1. Buenas noches. ____ 2. Buenas tardes. ____ 3. Buenos días. ____

a.
A.M.

b.
P.M.

c.
P.M.

**D** **Just as English speakers use abbreviations, Spanish speakers also abbreviate words. Here are a few examples:**

Señor - Sr.
Señora - Sra.
Señorita - Srta.

Note that the abbreviation "Ms." does not exist in Spanish.

**Address envelopes to the the following people in Spanish using abbreviations.**

1. Miss Alicia Salas _____

2. Mr. Juan Ayerbe _____

3. Mrs. Cecilia Guzmán _____

WELCOME TO SPANISH

**A** Decide who's saying what. Write the appropriate letter next to the illustration.

    **a.** ¡Hola!          **b.** Adiós.          **c.** Chao.

**1.** ____

**2.** ____

**3.** ____

**B** Tell if the following farewells are formal (F) or informal (I).

    **1.** Adiós, señor. ____    **2.** Hasta luego, Paco. ____

    **3.** Chao. ____    **4.** Hasta mañana, señora Morales. ____

**C** Say these Spanish words carefully.

    hola          hasta

There is one letter that you did not hear. It is not pronounced in Spanish.

    What letter is it? ____

Now say the following Spanish words.

    hotel          hospital

**WELCOME TO SPANISH**

## A Match the word with the picture.

**a.** una mesa       **b.** una silla       **c.** una mochila
**d.** una calculadora   **e.** un lápiz       **f.** un bolígrafo
**g.** un cuaderno    **h.** una goma

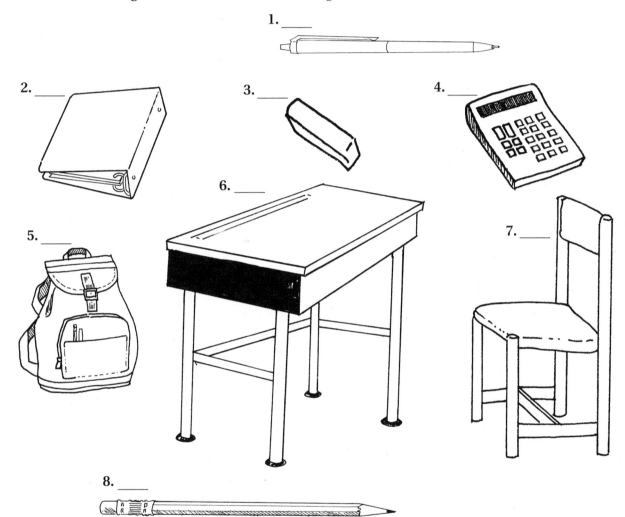

1. ____

2. ____

3. ____

4. ____

5. ____

6. ____

7. ____

8. ____

**B** Match the things that you usually use together.

A                                          B

1. una mesa y ____                         **a.** un bolígrafo

2. un lápiz y ____                         **b.** un borrador

3. una tiza y ____                         **c.** una goma

4. una hoja de papel y ____                **d.** una silla

**C** Circle the letter of the best follow-up to *por favor.*

1. Por favor.
   **a.** ¡Hola!
   **b.** Gracias.
   **c.** Chao.

**D** Write the missing letter of each word.

g____ma

t____za

bo____ígrafo

computado____a

____loc

Now put the missing letters together to form a word. _____

 # **4 Números**

**A** Write the number.

1. ocho     _____

2. dieciocho     _____

3. veintiocho     _____

4. ochenta y ocho     _____

5. ochocientos     _____

6. ocho mil     _____

**B** Write the number.

1. siete     _____

2. setenta     _____

3. setecientos     _____

4. nueve     _____

5. noventa     _____

6. novecientos     _____

7. cinco     _____

8. quince     _____

9. quinientos     _____

**C** Write down the following telephone numbers.

1. tres, cuarenta y cinco, setenta, ochenta y nueve

_____

2. cinco, treinta y tres, cuarenta y ocho, cincuenta

_____

**D** Write the following famous years in American and Spanish history.

    1. mil setecientos setenta y seis     _____

    2. mil cuatrocientos noventa y dos     _____

    3. mil novecientos treinta y seis     _____

**Use the years in Activity D to tell when these events happened.**

    1. el descubrimiento de América     _____

    2. la independencia de los Estados Unidos de América     _____

    3. la guerra civil española     _____

**E** Fill in the numbers, then connect the dots.

¿Qué animal es?

**a.** un tigre

**b.** un elefante

**c.** un león

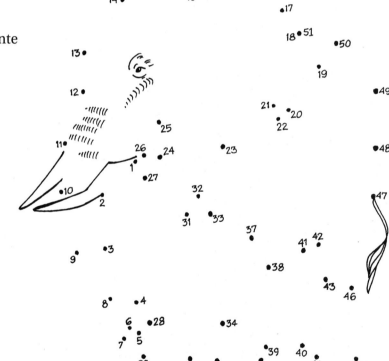

**8**     *Invitation to Languages*     © Copyright Glencoe/McGraw-Hill

**F** Write the letter of the name of the money.

    **a.** peseta         **b.** quetzal

    **c.** peso          **d.** sucre

1. ____

2. ____

3. ____

4. ____

*Números*     **9**

WELCOME TO SPANISH

#  5 La cortesía

**A  Circle the letter of the best response.**

1. ¡Hola!
   a. Adiós.
   b. ¡Hola! ¿Qué tal?
   c. De nada.

2. Gracias, señor.
   a. No hay de qué.
   b. Sí.
   c. Chao.

**B  Circle the letter of the best follow-up.**

1. Una hoja de papel, por favor.
   a. De nada.
   b. ¡Hola!
   c. Gracias.

**C  Circle the letter of the expression that doesn't fit.**

1. ¡Hola!
   a. Chao.
   b. Buenos días.
   c. Gracias.

2. Hasta luego.
   a. ¿Qué tal?
   b. Hasta pronto.
   c. Buenas noches.

3. Muy bien.
   a. Estupendo.
   b. Bien, gracias.
   c. ¿Y tú?

**D  Look at this menu in a Mexican restaurant. Work with a classmate. Each of you will tell what you are going to order. If you aren't sure what something is, find out from someone in the class. For example, you can ask: *¿Qué es un burrito?***

Café Tacuba

| | |
|---|---|
| Ensalada de tomate | 100 pesos |
| Guacamole | 100 pesos |
| Sopa de tortilla | 50 pesos |
| Taco | 250 pesos |
| Enchilada | 275 pesos |
| Burrito | 240 pesos |
| Tostada | 200 pesos |

**E**  Look at these pictures. Notice that each dish is called a *tortilla*. A *tortilla* in Mexico is a type of pancake made from either corn meal or flour. A *tortilla* in Spain is an egg omelette. A typical Spanish *tortilla* is called *una tortilla a la española.* It is an egg omelette made with potatoes and onions.

una tortilla

una tortilla a la española

*La cortesía*    **11**

WELCOME TO SPANISH

# 6 La hora

**A** **Match the time with each clock.**

a. Es la una.                        b. Son las dos y media.
c. Son las tres y veinte.            d. Son las diez y cuarto.
e. Son las once treinta y cinco.     f. Son las ocho menos veinte.

1. ____ 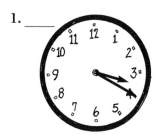   2. ____    3. ____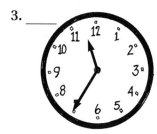

4. ____ 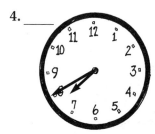   5. ____ 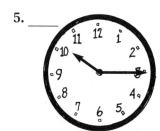   6. ____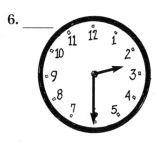

**B** **Match the expressions that mean the same thing.**

1. ____ Son las tres y media.        a. Son las tres (y) quince.

2. ____ Son las tres y cuarto.       b. Son las tres cuarenta y cinco.

3. ____ Son las tres menos cuarto.   c. Son las tres (y) treinta.

**C** **Fill out your class schedule in Spanish. Some subjects you may want to use are:**

matemáticas
inglés
español (lenguas)
historia (ciencias sociales)
ciencia (biología, física)
computadora (informática)
educación física
música
arte

| Hora | Clase |
| --- | --- |
|  |  |
|  |  |
|  |  |
|  |  |
|  |  |
|  |  |
|  |  |
|  |  |

#  Los colores

**A** What colors would you need to color the sky, the clouds, and the grass in a picture of a park on a beautiful spring day? Answer in Spanish.

_____

**B** Color this bird in at least three colors and label them in Spanish.

_____

**C** Design a flag for your school and color it. Label the colors in Spanish.

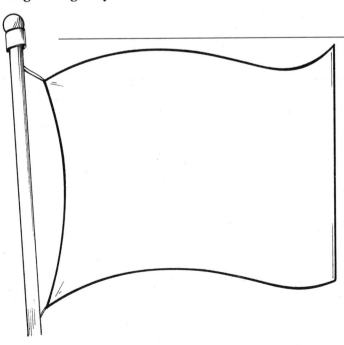

*Los colores*  **13**

# Los días de la semana

**A** Each of the following words has a missing letter. Write the missing letter.

vier____es

____unes

j____eves

miércole____

mart____s

Now unscramble the missing letters to spell a day of the week in Spanish.

_____

**B** In English, the days of the week are written with a capital letter. In Spanish, they are written with a small letter: *lunes, martes, miércoles, jueves, viernes, sábado, domingo.* Write a capital "A" next to the expression that means "capital letter" and a small "a" next to the expression that means "small letter."

una letra mayúscula ____

una letra minúscula ____

**C** Read the following.

En una semana hay siete días. Los siete días de la semana son: lunes, martes, miércoles, jueves, viernes, sábado y domingo.

In Spanish, the expression *ocho días* refers to a week. *Quince días* refers to two weeks. If there are seven days in a week, can you guess why Spanish speakers refer to the week as eight days and two weeks as fifteen days?

_____

_____

_____

_____

NAME _____   DATE _____

 **Los meses y las estaciones**

**A**  Complete the answers to the following questions.

1. ¿Cuántos meses hay en un año?

   Hay _____ meses en un año.

2. ¿Cuántos días hay en una semana?

   Hay _____ días en una semana.

3. ¿Cuántas estaciones hay en un año?

   Hay _____ estaciones en un año.

**B**  Choose the correct months.

1. los meses del invierno     ____        **a.** junio, julio y agosto

2. los meses de la primavera ____        **b.** marzo, abril y mayo

3. los meses del verano       ____        **c.** diciembre, enero y febrero

4. los meses del otoño        ____        **d.** septiembre, octubre y noviembre

**C**  Complete with true information.

Mi cumpleaños es en el mes de _____. La fecha de mi

cumpleaños es el ____ de _____.

**D**  Answer the following questions.

1. ¿Cuál es la fecha de hoy? _____

2. ¿Qué día es mañana? _____

**E**  Write the months and seasons when people usually do these activities.

1. el fútbol  _____

2. el béisbol _____

3. el esquí _____

WELCOME TO SPANISH

© Copyright Glencoe/McGraw-Hill          *Los meses y las estaciones*          **15**

# 10 El tiempo

**A** Write the letter of the sentence next to the picture that goes with it.

**a.** Está nevando.  **b.** Hace mucho frío.  **c.** Hace calor.
**d.** Hay sol.  **e.** Hace viento.

1. _____

2. _____

3. _____

5. _____

4. _____

**B** Circle the letters of the expressions that can be used to support the numbered sentences. There may be more than one answer.

**1.** Hace buen tiempo.
  **a.** Está lloviendo.
  **b.** Hay sol.
  **c.** Hace calor.
  **d.** Está nevando.
  **e.** El sol brilla.

**2.** Hace mal tiempo.
  **a.** Está lloviendo.
  **b.** Está nevando.
  **c.** Hay sol.
  **d.** Hace mucho frío.
  **e.** Hace un tiempo estupendo.

# 11 Yo soy...

**A** Write *sí* after each true sentence and *no* after each false one.

1. When Spanish speakers talk about themselves, they say *yo*. ____

2. When Spanish speakers speak to a friend, they say *tú*. ____

3. Spanish speakers use the same verb form with *yo* and *tú*. ____

**B** Complete the following conversations with *soy* or *eres*.

1. ¡Hola! ¿Quién _____?

¿Yo? Yo _____ José. José Garza.

2. ¡Hola! ¿Tú _____ Anita?

Sí, _____ Anita Torres.

Y tú, ¿quién _____?

**C** After you complete the conversations in Activity B, get together with a classmate. Perform the conversations together.

**A** Look at this map. Then circle the letter of the response that gives true information about you.

1. ¿Eres de los Estados Unidos?
   **a.** Sí, soy de los Estados Unidos.
   **b.** No, no soy de los Estados Unidos.

2. ¿Eres de Dallas?
   **a.** Sí, soy de Dallas.
   **b.** No, no soy de Dallas.

**If you answered no to either of the above questions, complete these sentences with true information.**

1. Yo no soy de los Estados Unidos. Soy de _____.

2. No soy de Dallas. Soy de _____.

**B** Underline the correct question word.

1. ¿(Quién, Qué) es?   2. ¿(Quién, Qué) es?   3. Soy Diego Martínez.
   Es Anita Salas.         Es una calculadora.      Perdón, ¿(quién, qué) eres?

4. Es Susana Dávila.                            5. Es una mochila.
   Perdón, ¿(quién, qué) es?                       Perdón, ¿(quién, qué) es?

**C** Answer the following questions about yourself. Girls will answer 1 to 3 and boys will answer 4 to 6.

1. ¿Quién eres?

_____

2. ¿Eres americana o mexicana?

_____

3. ¿De dónde eres?

_____

4. ¿Quién eres?

_____

5. ¿Eres americano o mexicano?

_____

6. ¿De dónde eres?

_____

**D** Complete these sentences with the letter *-o* or *-a.*

1. José es mexican____.

2. José no es american____.

3. Y Debbi es american____.

4. Debbi no es mexican____.

5. Yo soy _____.

Debbi

José

*Soy de...*   **19**

**E** **Complete the story using either *es, soy* or *eres*.**

David _____ americano. David no _____ mexicano. Pepe _____

mexicano. ¿Y tú? ¿Qué _____ ? ¿ _____ de los Estados Unidos?

Yo _____ de _____ (name of city or town).

**F** **Choose the correct question word.**

Qué                          Quién                          De dónde

**1.** ¿ _____ es?

**2.** ¡Hola! ¿ _____ eres?

**3.** ¿ _____ es Elena?

# 13 Hablo español

**A** Look at this map. Spanish is the language spoken in each of these countries. Can you name any of the capitals of these countries?

_____

_____

_____

_____

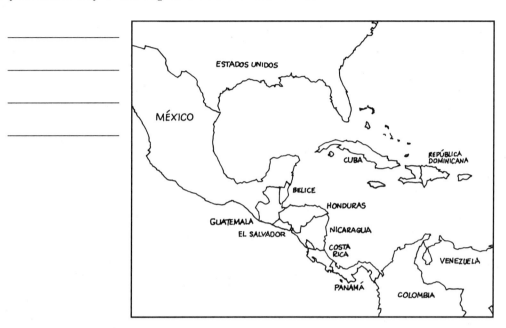

ESTADOS UNIDOS

MÉXICO

CUBA

REPÚBLICA DOMINICANA

BELICE

HONDURAS

GUATEMALA

EL SALVADOR

NICARAGUA

COSTA RICA

VENEZUELA

PANAMÁ

COLOMBIA

**B** Complete the answers to the following questions. Then work with a classmate. Ask and answer the questions together.

1. —¿Tú habl____ ruso?

   —No, yo no habl____ ruso.

   —¿No?

   —Yo, no. Pero Igor habl____ ruso.

2. —¿Habl____ inglés?

   —¿Quién? ¿Yo?

   —Sí, tú.

   —Sí, habl____ inglés. Habl____ inglés y español.

*Hablo español*     **21**

**C** Complete the sentences with question words that make sense.

1. ¿ _____ habla español?
   Ramona habla español.
   Ella es de la Argentina.

2. Y, ¿ _____ habla Antonio?
   Antonio habla italiano.
   Él es de Italia.

3. ¿ _____ habla inglés?
   Bill habla inglés.
   Él es de los Estados Unidos.
   Bill habla español también.

**D** Find the names of languages in the following puzzle. Circle each language you find. The name can be read from left to right, right to left, top to bottom, bottom to top, or diagonally.

**Word Bank**

| | |
|---|---|
| árabe | chino |
| español | francés |
| inglés | japonés |
| latín | polaco |
| ruso | |

```
V  L  A  P  O  L  A  C  O
O  X  L  O  Y  Z  Q  H  S
Y  S  É  L  G  N  I  I  U
J  O  T  A  L  I  M  N  R
A  A  E  C  E  Á  N  O  O
P  M  P  O  S  R  R  I  P
B  E  L  O  Ñ  A  P  S  E
L  A  T  I  N  B  C  L  R
F  R  A  N  C  É  S  G  T
O  L  L  O  E  L  S  E  E
```

When you have completed the puzzle, use the letters printed in boldface to form a word. The letters spell the name of a person.

___ ___ ___ ___ ___

Then change one letter in the name to make a new word.

___ ___ ___ ___ ___

# 14 Estudio...

**A** Match the subject with the book cover.

a. latín      b. historia      c. biología

d. música      e. geometría      f. arte

1. ____       2. ____

3. ____ 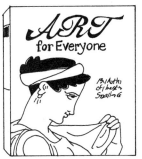      4. ____

5. ____       6. ____

**B** Complete each of the following words with the missing letters.

1. la esc ____ ____ la

2. yo estud ____ ____

3. la leng ____ ____

4. la c ____ ____ nc ____ ____

5. la histor ____ ____

**C** Look at the school schedule you wrote in Lesson 6 page 12 of the Workbook. Use it to complete this paragraph.

Yo estudio _____. La clase de _____ es a _____.

El profesor (La profesora) de _____ es el señor (la señora, la señorita)

_____.

**D** Some classes are easy *(fácil)* and others are difficult *(difícil).* Look at your schedule and rate all of your classes.

La clase de _____ es fácil.　　　La clase de _____ es fácil.

La clase de _____ es difícil.　　La clase de _____ es difícil.

**E** Complete the following conversation with the missing letters -*as* or -*o*.

—María, ¿estudi____ español?

—Sí, estudi____ español.

—¿Dónde estudi____ español?

—Pues, estudi____ español en la escuela.

—¿Es interesante la clase de español?

—Sí, es muy interesante. Y no es muy difícil.

—¿Tú habl____ mucho en la clase de español?

—Sí, mucho. Pero no habl____ inglés. Habl____ solamente en español.

**F** Now complete the following story about María by filling in the missing letters.

María estudi____ español. Estudi____ español en la escuela. La clase de

español es muy interesante. María habl____ mucho en la clase. Pero no

habl____ inglés. Sólo habl____ español.

# 15 Mi casa

WELCOME TO SPANISH

**A** Label the rooms of this house.

1. la sala          2. el comedor          3. la cocina
4. el cuarto de dormir     5. el cuarto de baño

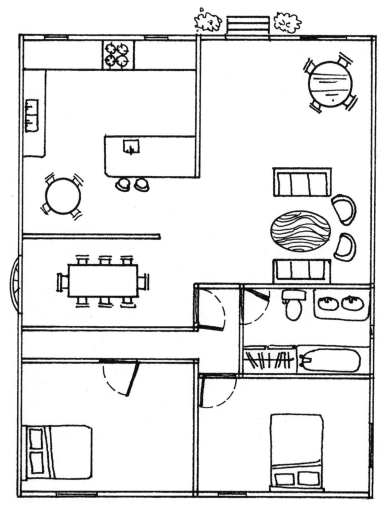

**B** Spanish is spoken in many countries. You will sometimes hear a different word used for the same thing depending upon where you are in the Spanish-speaking world. The word for "bedroom" is an example. If you use the term *cuarto de dormir,* everyone will understand you. But there are some other ways to say bedroom. They are:

el cuarto
la recámara
la habitación
el dormitorio

**C** Look at this house and write *sí* after each true sentence and *no* after each false one.

    **1.** Hay un carro en el garaje      ____

    **2.** Hay muchas rosas en el jardín.      ____

    **3.** Hay veinte cuartos en la casa.      ____

    **4.** Hay un jardín alrededor de la casa.      ____

**D** There are many Spanish words that are used in English. Read the following sentences and underline the Spanish words that are used in English.

Es una casa de adobe.
En el centro de la casa
    hay un patio.

**E** Underline the correct completion to this sentence.

          una casa pequeña.

**Hay muchos cuartos en**

          una casa grande.

**F** What room are these people in? Match the activities with the rooms.

    **1.** ____ José come.           **a.** el dormitorio, el cuarto de dormir

    **2.** ____ Elena toma un baño.     **b.** el comedor

    **3.** ____ Roberto duerme.       **c.** el cuarto de baño

WELCOME TO SPANISH

# 16 Mi familia

**A** Tell about your family. If you do not have one of the relatives, put an X in the blank.

1. Yo tengo _____ hermanos.

2. Yo tengo _____ hermanas.

3. Yo tengo _____ primos (y primas).

4. Yo tengo _____ tías.

5. Yo tengo _____ tíos.

**B** Choose the correct words to complete the following dictionary.

tío      primo      hermano      abuelo
tía      prima      hermana      abuela

1. _____ : un hermano de mi padre o madre

2. _____ : otro hijo de mi madre o padre

3. _____ : la madre de mi madre o padre

4. _____ : una hija de mi tío o tía

5. _____ : el padre de mi madre o padre

**C** Something is funny about the dictionary in Activity B. A dictionary always has the words in alphabetical order. Arrange the words in alphabetical order.

1. _____

2. _____

3. _____

4. _____

5. _____

**D** See how easy it is to guess at the meaning of words. Choose the correct word to complete each sentence.

1. El padre de mi padre es mi abuelo _____. (materno, paterno)

2. El padre de mi madre es mi abuelo _____. (materno, paterno)

**E** Underline the correct ending to this sentence.

una familia pequeña.

**Hay muchas personas en**

una familia grande.

**F** Complete the following with *tienes, tengo, tiene,* and any other words you may need. Then give true answers about yourself.

1. ¿ _____ (tú) una familia grande o pequeña?

Yo _____ una familia _____ .

Hay _____ personas en mi familia.

2. ¿ _____ hermanos?

Sí, yo _____ _____ hermanos.

(o) No, yo no _____ hermanos.

3. Si tú _____ hermanos, ¿cuántos hermanos _____ ?

Yo _____ _____ hermanos.

4. ¿Cuántos años _____ ?

¿Yo? Yo _____ _____ años.

5. Y tu hermano, ¿cuántos años _____ ?

Él _____ _____ años.   (o)   Yo no _____

hermano.

6. Y tu hermana, ¿cuántos años _____ ?

Ella _____ _____ años.   (o)   Yo no _____ hermana.

**G** Work with a classmate. Make up a story using the information from Activity F. Tell your stories to each other.

# 17 Mi mascota

**A** On a separate sheet of paper, draw a picture of a pet store. Then work with a classmate and have a conversation about buying a pet. Use a separate sheet of paper for your drawing.

**B** Write *sí* after each true sentence and *no* after each false one.

1. Un canario es un pájaro. ____

2. Un gerbo es un pájaro también. ____

3. Un perro es un animal doméstico. ____

4. Un elefante es un animal doméstico también. ____

5. Un tigre es un animal salvaje. ____

6. Un león es de la misma familia que un gato. ____

7. Una víbora es un reptil. ____

8. Un pez dorado es un reptil también. ____

**C** Answer these questions about yourself.

1. ¿Te interesa la historia?

_____

2. ¿Te gusta la clase de historia?

_____

3. ¿Te gusta mucho o un poco?

_____

4. ¿Te interesan las matemáticas?

_____

5. ¿Te gusta la clase de matemáticas?

_____

_____

**6.** ¿Te gusta mucho o un poco?

_____

**D** **Complete these sentences with *-a* or *-an*.**

Me gust____ los animales. Me gust____ mucho. Yo tengo una mascota.

Tengo un perro. Me encant____ mi perro. Es adorable.

Yo tengo un acuario también. En mi acuario hay pececillos.

Los pececillos me interes____ mucho.

**E** **Match the activity in the picture with the word.**

**a.** salta      **b.** juega      **c.** nada      **d.** canta      **e.** habla

**1.** ____

**2.** ____

**3.** ____

**4.** ____

**5.** ____

**F** **Complete the following sentences.**

**1.** El canario canta y yo cant____ también.

**2.** El perro salt____ y yo salt____ también.

**3.** El pececillo nad____ y yo nad____ también.

**4.** El papagayo habl____ y yo habl____ también.

**5.** El gato jueg____ y yo jueg____ también.

# 18 Los deportes

**A** Place the number where it belongs in the illustration.

1. el campo          2. el jugador
3. el balón          4. el equipo

**B** Complete the following words.

1. el vóli_____     2. el béis_____

3. el fút_____      4. el básquet_____

**C** Here are some words used in talking about sports. Can you guess what they mean? Tell which sport they go with.

**a.** el béisbol          **b.** el tenis          **c.** el fútbol

1. ____ el gol          2. ____ el foul          3. ____ el bate

4. ____ el pícher       5. ____ el jonrón        6. ____ la base

7. ____ la raqueta

**D** Write *sí* after each true sentence and *no* after each false one.

1. El pícher es un jugador de béisbol. ____

2. El béisbol es un deporte muy popular en los Estados Unidos. ____

3. El jugador de fútbol juega béisbol. ____

4. Hay once jugadores en el equipo de fútbol. ____

5. El jugador de tenis o el tenista juega con una raqueta. ____

6. Hay cien jugadores en un equipo de básquetbol. ____

**E** Answer these questions about yourself.

1. ¿Te gustan los deportes?

_____

2. ¿Te gusta el béisbol?

_____

3. ¿Te gusta el fútbol?

_____

4. ¿Te gusta el básquetbol?

_____

5. ¿Qué deporte te gusta más?

_____

#  La ropa

**A** Draw a person. Then label his or her clothing.

**B** Put an X by the clothing items that both boys and girls can wear.

1. los tenis ____

2. la falda ____

3. la sudadera ____

4. el pantalón ____

5. la blusa ____

6. el blue jean ____

NAME _____  DATE _____

**C  Answer these questions about yourself.**

1. ¿Tienes un par de tenis?

_____

2. ¿Llevas los tenis a la escuela?

_____

3. ¿Tienes una sudadera?

_____

4. ¿Llevas la sudadera en el gimnasio?

_____

5. ¿Tienes un gorro?

_____

6. ¿Llevas el gorro en la sala de clase?

_____

**Notice that you will hear both *el gorro* and *la gorra*.**
el gorro             la gorra

# A Let's Read in Spanish!

**A** You'll be surprised at how much Spanish you are able to read. Let's give it a try and find out how easy it really is.

## España

España es un país. Está en el continente de Europa. España y Portugal forman una península—la península ibérica. Es una península porque tiene agua a los tres lados. Al este y al sur está el mar Mediterráneo. Al oeste está el océano Atlántico.

Los Pirineos están al norte. Los Pirineos son montañas altas. Las montañas forman una frontera natural entre España y Francia.

La capital de España es Madrid. Madrid está en el centro del país. Barcelona es otra ciudad importante de España. Barcelona es una ciudad industrial.

**B** Words that look alike and sound alike in two languages are called cognates. There are many cognates in this reading selection. Match the following cognates.

| | | |
|---|---|---|
| 1. ____ continente | **a.** mountains | |
| 2. ____ península | **b.** form | |
| 3. ____ Europa | **c.** industrial | |
| 4. ____ forman | **d.** important | |
| 5. ____ este | **e.** peninsula | |
| 6. ____ norte | **f.** center | |
| 7. ____ océano | **g.** ocean | |
| 8. ____ montañas | **h.** Europe | |
| 9. ____ importante | **i.** frontier (border) | |
| 10. ____ frontera | **j.** east | |
| 11. ____ industrial | **k.** north | |
| 12. ____ centro | **l.** continent | |

*Let's Read in Spanish!*

**C** Choose the correct completion to each statement.

1. España es _____.

   **a.** un continente    **b.** un país    **c.** una península

2. España y _____ forman una península.

   **a.** Francia    **b.** Barcelona    **c.** Portugal

3. _____ tiene agua a los tres lados.

   **a.** Una península    **b.** Un país    **c.** Un continente

4. _____ es la capital de España.

   **a.** Barcelona    **b.** Madrid    **c.** Sevilla

5. El Mediterráneo es _____.

   **a.** un mar    **b.** un océano    **c.** una montaña

# B Reading about Science

**A** Read the following passage about biology. You'll be amazed how easy it is.

La biología es una ciencia. Es la ciencia que estudia las plantas y los animales. El biólogo es el científico que estudia la biología. El biólogo o la bióloga trabaja en un laboratorio. Para sus investigaciones usa un microscopio. En el microscopio observa y estudia células, bacteria y virus.

**B** In the reading selection, find a word that is related to each of the following words.

1. el biólogo _____

2. la ciencia _____

3. el estudio _____

4. la observación _____

5. celular _____

6. viral _____

# Welcome to *French!*

# 1 Les salutations

**A** Circle the letter of the best response.

1. Salut!
   a. Merci.
   b. Ça va bien.
   c. Salut!

2. Ça va?
   a. Ça va.
   b. Et toi?
   c. Salut!

3. Ça va. Et toi?
   a. Et toi?
   b. Ça va?
   c. Ça va bien, merci.

**B** In the illustrations below, which people are probably saying *Salut* and which are probably saying *Bonjour?* Write A for those saying *Salut!* and B for those saying *Bonjour.*

1. ____

2. ____

3. ____

**C** Just as English speakers use abbreviations, French speakers also abbreviate words. Here are few examples:

| | |
|---|---|
| Monsieur | M. |
| Madame | Mme |
| Mademoiselle | Mlle |

Note that the abbreviation "Ms." does not exist in French.

**Address the envelopes to the following people in French using abbreviations.**

1. Miss Briand
2. Mr. Benoît
3. Mrs. Chandelier

1.

2.

3.

**D** **Circle the expressions that have approximately the same meaning.**

1. Ça va.
2. Salut!
3. Ça va bien.
4. Bien, merci.
5. Et toi?
6. Pas mal!

*Les salutations*

#  Au revoir

**A** Decide who's saying what. Write the appropriate letter next to the illustration.

    **a.** Au revoir.        **b.** Ciao.        **c.** Salut!

**1.** ____

**2.** ____

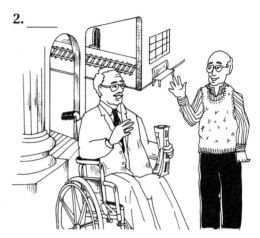

**3.** ____

**B** Choose the farewell you are going to use in each of the following situations. Write the letter that corresponds to the expression you choose.

    **a.** Au revoir.        **b.** Ciao.
    **c.** À bientôt.       **d.** À demain.

**1.** You're saying "goodbye" to someone you plan to see tomorrow. ____

**2.** You're saying "goodbye" to an adult who's about to leave on a trip. ____

**3.** You're saying "so long" to a good friend. ____

**4.** You're saying "bye" to someone you plan on seeing again soon. ____

**C** Look at the "farewells" in Activity B. Which one means almost the same thing as *À tout à l'heure?*

_____

_____

NAME _____ DATE _____

# 3 En classe

**A** **Match the word with the picture.**

    **a.** une calculatrice    **b.** un crayon    **c.** une table

    **d.** une feuille de papier  **e.** un ordinateur    **f.** une chaise

    **g.** un stylo-bille    **h.** un livre

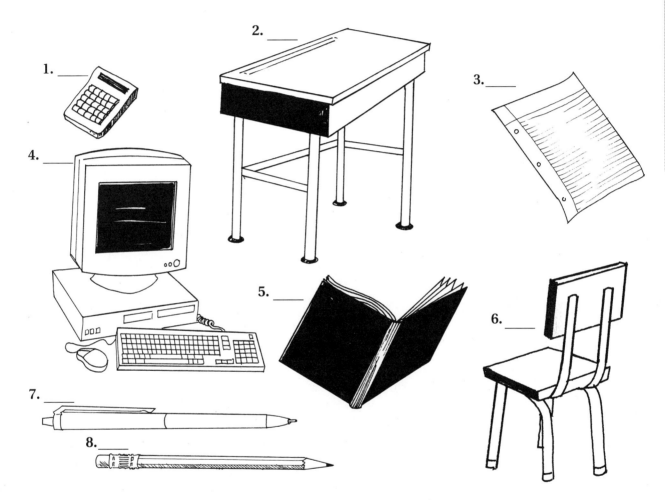

**B** **Write the missing letter in each word.**

un ____rayon        une t____ble        une c____aise

un pup____tre        une calculatric____       un liv____e

**Now put the missing letters together to form a word.** _____

**C** **Choose the items you need.**

**a.** une feuille de papier    **f.** une calculatrice
**b.** un livre    **g.** un ordinateur
**c.** un sac à dos    **h.** un morceau de craie
**d.** un crayon    **i.** une table
**e.** une gomme

1. _____ You are going to write a composition for your Language Arts class.

2. _____ You have lots of books and things to carry to school.

3. _____ You want to spread out materials to do a drawing.

4. _____ You are going to write something on the blackboard.

5. _____ You are going to solve an arithmetic problem with the help of a machine.

6. _____ You are going to do an arithmetic problem without a machine.

**D** **Write the missing letters in each word.**

1. un cah_____

2. un morc_____ de cr_____

3. une ch_____ se

4. une f_____ lle de pap_____

5. un ordinat_____

 **4** **L**es nombres

**A** **Write the number.**

1. trois       _____

2. treize       _____

3. trente       _____

4. trois cents       _____

5. trois cent trois       _____

6. trois mille       _____

7. six       _____

8. seize       _____

9. soixante-six       _____

10. six cents       _____

11. six cent soixante       _____

12. six mille       _____

13. huit       _____

14. dix-huit       _____

15. quatre-vingts       _____

16. quatre-vingt-huit       _____

17. huit cents       _____

18. huit cent quatre-vingt-huit       _____

**B** **Write the following famous years in American and French history.**

1. dix-sept cent soixante-dix-sept       _____

2. quatorze cent quatre-vingt-douze       _____

3. dix-sept cent quatre-vingt-dix-huit       _____

*Les nombres*     **43**

Match the historical event with the year indicated above.

**1.** l'arrivé de Christophe Colomb au nouveau monde        _____

**2.** l'indépendance des États-Unis d'Amérique        _____

**3.** la Révolution Française        _____

**C** **Write the letter next to the name of the money.**

**a.** deux dollars canadiens
**b.** cinquante francs français
**c.** vingt francs français

**1.** ____

**2.** ____

**3.** ____

*Invitation to Languages*        © Copyright Glencoe/McGraw-Hill

# ❀5❀ *La politesse*

**A** Who's saying what? Write the letter in the space provided.

**a.** Je vous en prie.

**b.** Merci.

**B** You're in a café ordering something to drink. You want to be polite. Choose the correct completion to your statement.

**1.** Un Schweppes, ____.
  **a.** merci
  **b.** je vous en prie
  **c.** s'il vous plaît

**2.** C'est combien le Schweppes, ____?
  **a.** merci
  **b.** je vous en prie
  **c.** s'il vous plaît

**C** Choose the expressions being used between the speakers in each picture.

**a.** Je vous en prie.
**b.** Je t'en prie.
**c.** S'il vous plaît.
**d.** S'il te plaît.

**D** Look at this menu from a French café. Work with a classmate. Each of you will decide what you are going to order.

**L'Affaire**

| | |
|---|---|
| Soupe à l'oignon | 30 F |
| Salade verte | 25 F |
| Pâté | 35 F |
| Pizza | 45 F |
| Spaghetti | 40 F |
| Omelette | 40 F |
| Sandwich au fromage | 45 F |
| Sandwich au jambon | 50 F |
| Sandwich au poulet | 50 F |
| Steak frites | 60 F |
| Crêpe | 30 F |
| Tarte aux fruits | 30 F |
| Glace au chocolat | 20 F |
| Sorbet | 25 F |

WELCOME TO FRENCH

## 6 L'heure

**A**  Match the time with each clock.

   **a.** Il est une heure.
   **b.** Il est deux heures trente. Il est deux heures et demie.
   **c.** Il est sept heures quarante.
   **d.** Il est dix heures quinze.
   **e.** Il est trois heures vingt.
   **f.** Il est onze heures trente-cinq.

1. _____   2. _____   3. _____

4. _____   5. _____   6. _____

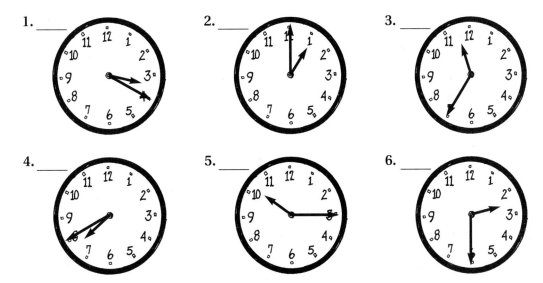

**B**  Write out the time for each event.

   **1.** Le concert est à deux heures et demie.        _____

   **2.** Le film est à huit heures quarante.           _____

   **3.** Le dîner est à sept heures trente.            _____

   **4.** Le show commence à huit heures quinze.        _____

# 7 Les couleurs

**A** What colors would you need to color the sky, the clouds, and the grass in a picture of a park on a beautiful spring day? Answer in French.

_____

**B** Color this bird in at least three colors and label them in French.

_____

**C** The French and American flags are the same colors. The colors, however, are given in reverse order when describing the flags. When we describe the American flag, we say it is red, white, and blue. The French say their flag is blue, white, and red. Based on this information, complete the following sentences correctly.

1. Le drapeau américain est _____, _____ et _____.

2. Le drapeau français est _____, _____ et _____.

WELCOME TO FRENCH

# Les jours de la semaine

**A** Write the missing letter of each word.

____ercredi

s____medi

vend____edi

lun____i

jeud____

Now put together the missing letters to spell a day of the week in French.

_____

**B** In English, the days of the week are written with a capital letter. In French, they are written with a small letter: *lundi, mardi, mercredi, jeudi, vendredi, samedi, dimanche.* Write a capital "A" next to the expression that means "capital letter," and a small "a" next to the expression that means "small letter".

une lettre majuscule    ____

une lettre minuscule    ____

**C** Read the following.

Il y a sept jours dans une semaine. Les jours de la semaine sont lundi, mardi, mercredi, jeudi, vendredi, samedi et dimanche.

In French, the expression *huit jours* refers to a week. *Quinze jours* refers to two weeks. If there are seven days in a week, explain why French speakers refer to the week as having eight days and two weeks as having fifteen days.

_____

_____

_____

_____

_____

# Les mois et les saisons

**A** Complete the answers to the following questions.

1. Il y a combien de mois dans une année?

Il y a _____ mois dans une année.

2. Il y a combien de jours dans une semaine?

Il y a _____ jours dans une semaine.

3. Il y a combien de saisons dans une année?

Il y a _____ saisons dans une année.

**B** Choose the correct months.

1. ____ les mois d'hiver

2. ____ les mois du printemps

3. ____ les mois d'été

4. ____ les mois d'automne

a. juin, juillet et août      b. mars, avril et mai
c. décembre, janvier et février      d. septembre, octobre et novembre

**C** Complete each statement with the appropriate months.

1. Il y a 28 jours au mois de _____.

2. Il y a 30 jours aux mois d'_____.

3. Et il y a trente et un jours aux mois de_____.

**D** **Complete with true information.**

Mon anniversaire est au mois

de _____ (au mois d'___).

La date de mon anniversaire c'est le _____.

**E** **Answer the following questions according to the calendar.**

| dimanche | lundi | mardi | mercredi | jeudi | vendredi | samedi |
|---|---|---|---|---|---|---|
| 30 | 31 | 1 | 2 | 3 | 4 | 5 |
| | | | | | | |

**1.** Aujourd'hui c'est quel jour?

_____

**2.** Et demain, c'est quel jour?

_____

**F** **Write in French the months and seasons when people do these activities.**

**1.** le baseball _____

_____

**2.** le football _____

_____

**3.** le ski _____

_____

*Les mois et les saisons*

# 10 L*e temps*

**A** Write the number of the sentence next to the picture that goes with it.

**1.** Il neige.  **2.** Il fait très froid.  **3.** Il fait chaud.
**4.** Il y a du soleil.  **5.** Il y a du vent.

a. _____

b. _____

c. _____

e. _____

d. _____

**B** Circle the letter of the expressions that can be used to support the numbered sentences. There may be more than one answer.

**1.** Il fait beau.
  **a.** Il pleut.
  **b.** Il y a du soleil.
  **c.** Il fait chaud.
  **d.** Il neige.
  **e.** Il y a du vent.

**2.** Il fait mauvais.
  **a.** Il pleut.
  **b.** Il neige.
  **c.** Il y a du soleil.
  **d.** Il fait très, très froid.
  **e.** Il fait un temps splendide.

*Invitation to Languages*

# Je suis...

**A** **Circle the correct choice.**

1. A French person uses _____ when speaking about himself or herself.
   **a.** tu                    **b.** je

2. A French person uses _____ when addressing or talking to a friend.
   **a.** tu                    **b.** je

**B** **Complete the following conversations with *tu es* or *je suis*.**

1. —Salut! _____ _____ une amie de Jean Paul, n'est-ce pas?

   —Oui, _____ _____ une amie de Jean Paul. _____ _____

   Thérèse Lepoint.

2. —Salut! _____ _____ un ami de Serge, n'est-ce pas?

   —Oui. _____ _____ un ami de Serge.

   _____ _____ Hervé. Et toi? _____ _____

   Nathalie Dumas, n'est-ce pas?

*Je suis...*     **53**

**C**  After you complete the conversations in Activity B, get together with a classmate. Perform the conversations together.

**D**  Answer the following question.

Tu t'appelles comment?

Je m'appelle _____.

**E**  You will notice as you study French that many words are spelled differently, even though they are pronounced the same. Two examples are:

un ami                    une amie

1. Underline the correct completion to each statement.
   **a.** *Une amie* refers to a (girl, boy).
   **b.** *Un ami* refers to a (girl, boy).

2. Complete each sentence.

   **a.** Robert est _____ _____ de Jean Claude.

   **b.** Émilie est _____ _____ de Jean Claude aussi.

**A** Circle the appropriate completions to the following conversations.

1. —Tu es d'où, Charles?
   —Moi, je suis de Paris.
   Ah, tu es _____. (français, américain)

2. —Tu es d'où, Carole?
   —Moi, je suis de New York.
   Ah, tu es _____. (française, américaine)

**B** Select the correct question word and write it in the blank.

*Qui*                          *D'où*

—_____ est un ami de Christian?

—Robert.

—Il est _____, Robert?

—Robert est de New York.

—Ah, il est américain.

**B** Complete the following words with *e* when necessary.

1. Nathalie est français____.

2. Et Paul est français____ aussi.

3. Robert est américain____.

4. Et Susanne est américain____ aussi.

5. Susanne est une ami____ de Robert.

6. Et Robert est un ami____ de Nathalie et Paul.

7. Moi, je suis américain____.

# Je parle français

**A**  Look at this map. French is the language spoken in each of these countries. How many of the capitals listed below can you match with their country?

1. Bamako          _____

2. Bruxelles       _____

3. Rabat           _____

4. Abidjan         _____

5. Dakar           _____

6. Paris           _____

7. Tunis           _____

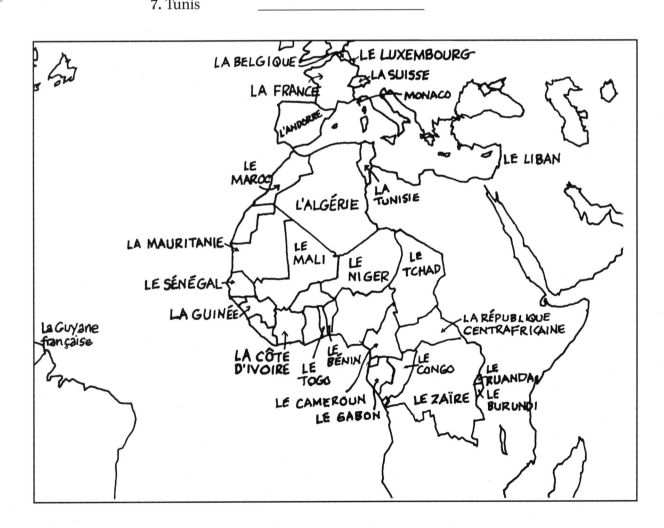

**C** **Choose the correct question word to complete each statement.**

*Qui*                      *D'où*

1. —_____ parle français?

   —Michel parle français.

   —Ah oui? Il est _____?

   —Michel est de Marseille.

2. —_____ parle italien?

   —Gianni parle italien.

   —Ah oui?

   —Oui, il est de Venise.

   —Il est_____?

   —De Venise.

3. —_____ parle anglais?

   —Annette parle anglais.

   —Ah, oui. Elle est de New York,

      n'est-ce pas?

   —Non.

   —Elle est _____, alors?

   —Annette est de Boston.

*Je parle français*     **57**

WELCOME TO FRENCH

**D** Find the names of the languages in the following puzzle. Circle each language you find. The name can be read from left to right, right to left, top to bottom, bottom to top, or diagonally.

```
J  A  P  O  N  A  I  S  O  Q  F  P  A  J
N  K  O  N  S  U  B  Y  T  Z  L  S  C  A
T  V  R  S  E  L  W  B  O  T  C  I  E  R
W  I  T  A  L  I  E  N  G  W  Q  A  S  M
E  V  U  R  D  X  M  K  S  P  H  D  S  T
K  I  G  T  P  N  Z  A  U  D  É  N  U  S
S  I  A  Ç  N  A  R  F  N  E  B  A  R  A
I  Q  I  G  M  N  D  T  Z  T  R  L  J  V
O  E  S  P  A  G  N  O  L  K  E  R  D  P
N  R  Z  S  P  L  P  M  X  F  U  I  D  Z
I  R  C  S  I  A  N  O  L  O  P  G  V  R
H  W  U  R  Y  I  Z  E  V  T  K  O  Q  X
C  E  R  G  B  S  U  P  Z  R  D  K  E  I
```

**Word Bank**

| | | |
|---|---|---|
| grec | portugais | russe |
| chinois | polonais | hébreu |
| arabe | anglais | italien |
| vietnamien | espagnol | français |
| japonais | | |

When you have completed the puzzle, use the bold letters to form a French word.

___  ___  ___  ___  ___

 J'aime...

**A** Match the subject with the book cover.

| | | |
|---|---|---|
| **a.** le latin | **b.** l'histoire | **c.** la biologie |
| **d.** la musique | **e.** la géographie | **f.** l'art |

1. ____

2. ____

3. ____

4. ____

5. ____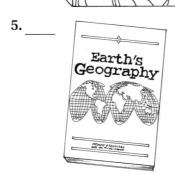

6. ____

**B** Complete each of the following words with the missing letters.

1. l'ar____    2. le françai____    3. l'anglai____    4. le moi____

5. juille____    6. chau____    7. mauvai____    8. je sui____

**C** Now pronounce the words from Activity B. Notice that the letters that you added are not pronounced. As you learn to spell in French, you will note that there are many letters that are not pronounced.

**D** List the classes you like and don't like.

1. J'aime _____.

2. Je n'aime pas _____.

**E** Complete the following sentences with the negative.

1. Je suis américain(e). Je _____ suis_____ français(e).

2. Je parle français. Je _____ parle _____ espagnol.

3. Il fait chaud. Il _____ fait _____ froid.

4. Il neige. Il _____ pleut _____.

**F** Complete the following sentences with the negative.

1. Jean est français. Il _____ est _____ américain.

2. Jean est de Nice. Il _____ est _____ de Paris.

3. Jean aime les maths. Il _____ aime _____ la biologie.

4. Moi, j'aime _____. Je _____ aime _____ _____.

# 15 Ma maison

**A** Label the rooms of this house.

1. le salon      2. la cuisine      3. la chambre
4. la salle à manger      5. la salle de bains

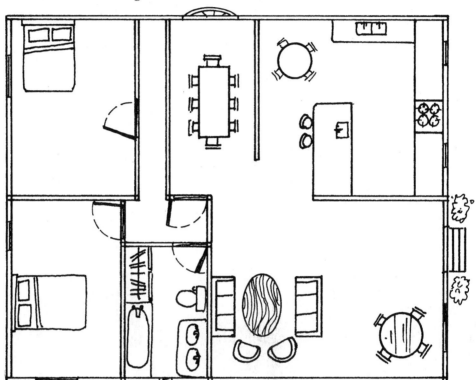

**B** Indicate if the following statements are *vrai* (V) or *faux* (F).

1. ____ Il y a une voiture dans le garage.

2. ____ Il y a un jardin autour de la maison.

3. ____ Il y a vingt pièces dans la maison.

4. ____ Il y a des roses dans le jardin.

*Ma maison*      **61**

**C** Choose the correct word to complete each sentence.

*petite*                     *grande*

Il y a quatre pièces dans une _____ maison. Il y a douze pièces

dans une_____ maison.

**D** Guess what room Jean-Claude is in.

*la cuisine*        *la salle à manger*    *la salle de bains*    *le garage*

1. Jean-Claude is working on his car.        _____

2. Jean-Claude is preparing a sandwich.      _____

3. Jean-Claude is having dinner.             _____

4. Jean-Claude is taking a shower.           _____

# 16 *Ma famille*

**A** **Circle the statement that is true for you.**

1. **a.** J'ai un frère.
   **b.** J'ai des frères.
   **c.** Je n'ai pas de frère.

2. **a.** J'ai une soeur.
   **b.** J'ai des soeurs.
   **c.** Je n'ai pas de soeur.

3. **a.** J'ai un cousin.
   **b.** J'ai des cousins.
   **c.** Je n'ai pas de cousin.

4. **a.** J'ai une tante.
   **b.** J'ai des tantes.
   **c.** Je n'ai pas de tante.

**B** **Tell about your family and relatives. If you do not have any, put an X in the blank.**

1. J'ai ____ (frère, frères).

2. J'ai ____ (soeur, soeurs).

3. J'ai ____ (cousin, cousins).

4. J'ai ____ (oncle, oncles).

5. J'ai ____ (tante, tantes).

**C** **Answer the following questions about yourself.**

1. Tu as une grande famille ou une petite famille?

   _____

2. Il y a combien de personnes dans ta famille?

   _____

3. Tu as une grande maison ou une petite maison?

   _____

4. Il y a combien de pièces dans ta maison?

   _____

**D** See how easy it is to guess at the meaning of words. Circle the correct word to complete each statement.

1. Le père de mon père est mon grand-père _____ .(maternel, paternel)

2. Le père de ma mère est mon grand-père _____. (maternel, paternel)

**E** Complete the following sentences with *as, ai,* or *a.* Then give true answers about yourself.

1. Tu ____ une grande famille ou une petite famille?

Moi, j'____ une _____ famille.

Il y a _____ personnes dans ma famille.

2. Tu ____ des frères?

Oui, j'_____ des frères. (ou) Non, je n'____ pas de frère.

3. Tu ____ quel âge?

Moi, j'____ _____ ans.

4. Et ton frère? Il ____ quel âge?

Mon frère ____ _____ ans. (ou) Je n'____ pas de frère.

5. Et ta soeur? Elle ____ quel âge?

Ma soeur ____ _____ ans. (ou) Moi, je n'____ pas de soeur.

**F** Work with a classmate. Make up a story using the information from Activity E. Tell your story to each other.

# 17 Un bon ami

**A** On a separate sheet of paper, draw a picture of a pet store. Then work with a classmate and have a conversation together about buying a pet.

**B** Indicate if the following statements are *vrai* (V) or *faux* (F).

1. ____ Le canari est un oiseau.

2. ____ La gerboise est un oiseau aussi.

3. ____ Le chien est un animal domestique.

4. ____ L'éléphant est un autre animal domestique.

5. ____ Le tigre est un animal sauvage.

6. ____ Le lion est de la même famille que le chat.

7. ____ Un serpent est un reptile.

8. ____ Un poisson rouge est un reptile aussi.

**C** Match the activity in the picture with the word.

**a.** il chante      **b.** il nage      **c.** elle parle      **d.** il saute

1. ____

2. ____

3. ____

4. ____

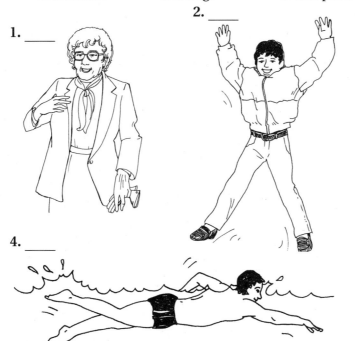

**D** Choose the correct animal to complete each statement and write it in the blank.

le chat          la perruche          le poisson          le canari

1. _____ chante.

2. _____ parle.

3. _____ saute.

4. _____ nage.

**E** Fill in the missing letters to complete the word for an animal.

1. ____anari

2. perruc____e

3. ois____au

4. gerbo____se

5. serpe____t

Now use the letters to spell the name of an animal.

_____

WELCOME TO FRENCH

# 18 Les sports

**A** Place the number where it belongs in the illustration.

1. le terrain
2. le joueur
3. l'équipe
4. le ballon

**B** Rewrite the following words in their shortened forms.

1. le foot(ball) _____

2. le volley(-ball) _____

3. le basket(-ball) _____

**C** Here are some words related to sports. Can you guess what they mean? Indicate the sports with which they are associated.

**a.** le base(-ball)        **b.** le foot(ball)        **c.** le tennis

1. la défense _____

2. le bâton _____

3. le serveur _____

4. la raquette _____

5. l'attaque _____

**D** Tell if the following statements about sports are *vrai* (V) or *faux* (F).

1. ____ Le foot est un sport d'équipe.

2. ____ Le baseball est un sport individuel. Il n'y a pas d'équipe.

3. ____ Il y a onze joueurs dans une équipe de football.

4. ____ Il y a cent joueurs dans une équipe de basketball.

# 19 Les vêtements

**A**  On a separate sheet of paper, draw a person. Draw his or her clothing. Then label what he or she is wearing.

**B**  Put an X by the clothes that boys and girls can wear.

1. les tennis ____          2. un pantalon ____

3. un (blue) jean ____      4. une blouse ____

5. un pull ____             6. une jupe ____

7. un blouson ____          8. une casquette ____

**C**  Answer these questions about yourself.

1. Tu as une paire de tennis?

_____

2. Tu portes les tennis à l'école?

_____

3. Tu as un sweat-shirt?

_____

4. Tu portes un sweat-shirt au gymnase?

_____

5. Tu as une casquette?

_____

6. Tu portes une casquette en classe?

_____

_____

#  Let's Read in French!

**A** You will be surprised at how much French you are able to read.
Let's give it a try and find out how easy it really is.

### La France

 L'Europe est un continent. La France est un pays. La France est en Europe. Paris est la capitale de la France. Il y a beaucoup de monuments fameux à Paris—la tour Eiffel, le Louvre, Notre Dame.

Lille est une ville importante de la France. Lille est une ville industrielle. Il y a beaucoup d'industrie à Lille.

Il y a des montagnes en France. Les Alpes sont dans l'est et les Pyrénées sont dans le sud.

**B** Words that look alike and sound alike in both languages are cognates. Find the French cognate for the following words.

1. Europe _____
2. capital _____
3. continent _____
4. monument _____
5. east _____
6. mountains _____
7. important _____
8. industrial _____

**C** Choose the correct completion to each statement.

1. La France est _____.
   **a.** un continent      **b.** un pays      **c.** une péninsule

2. Les Pyrénées sont des _____.
   **a.** montagnes      **b.** lacs      **c.** mers

3. Lille est une ville _____.
   **a.** industrielle      **b.** pittoresque      **c.** tropicale

4. La tour Eiffel est _____ de Paris.
   **a.** une montagne      **b.** une ville      **c.** un monument

# Reading about Biology

**A** Read the following passage about biology. You'll be amazed how easy it is.

La biologie est une science. La biologie est la science qui étudie les plantes et les animaux. Un biologiste ou une biologiste étudie la biologie. Un (une) biologiste travaille dans un laboratoire. Il (Elle) utilise un microscope pour faire des recherches. Dans le microscope il (elle) observe, étudie et analyse les cellules, les bactéries et les virus.

**B** Read this selection once again and find all the cognates.

_____

_____

_____

_____

**C** Many words are related to one another because they come from the same root. For example, the words *la biologie* and *le (la) biologiste* are related. In the reading selection, find words that are related to the following.

**1.** un biologiste _____

**2.** une étude _____

**3.** une observation _____

**4.** cellulaire _____

**5.** bactérien _____

**6.** viral _____

# Welcome to Italian!

 **Ciao!**

**A** Look at the two illustrations. Write A or B to indicate in which conversation each expression is being used.

1. ____ Buon giorno.  2. ____ Come stai?

3. ____ Come sta?  4. ____ Ciao!

5. ____ Bene, grazie. E tu?  6. ____ Bene, grazie. E Lei?

A.

B.

**B** Circle the letter of the best response.

1. Ciao!
   a. Ciao!
   b. E tu?
   c. Grazie.

2. Come stai?
   a. Bene, grazie. E Lei?
   b. Bene, grazie. E tu?
   c. Ciao, grazie.

3. Buon giorno.
   a. Grazie. E Lei?
   b. Buon giorno.
   c. Buona sera.

**C** Number the following in order from "so so" to "really great, fabulous."

____ Abbastanza bene.  ____ Benissimo.

____ Così, così.  ____ Bene.

____ Molto bene.

WELCOME TO ITALIAN

#  2 *A**rrivederci!*

**A** Choose the correct responses you would use in taking leave of someone.

    1. an older person you hardly know
       **a.** Ciao!
       **b.** Ci vediamo.
       **c.** ArrivederLa.

    2. a close friend your own age
       **a.** Ciao!
       **b.** ArrivederLa.
       **c.** Arrivederci.

    3. someone you're going to see again the same day
       **a.** A domani.
       **b.** Arrivederci.
       **c.** A più tardi.

    4. someone you're going to see again really soon
       **a.** A presto.
       **b.** Arrivederci.
       **c.** ArrivederLa.

    5. someone you plan to see again tomorrow
       **a.** A più tardi.
       **b.** A domani.
       **c.** Ciao.

**B** Complete the following words with the correct letters. Then pronounce the words carefully.

    1. Arriveder____ ____.

    2. ____ ____ vediamo.

    3. ____ ____ ao.

#  In classe

**A** Match the word with the illustration.

- **a.** una calcolatrice
- **b.** una sedia
- **c.** un quaderno
- **d.** una matita
- **e.** una penna
- **f.** un tavolo
- **g.** uno zaino
- **h.** una gomma

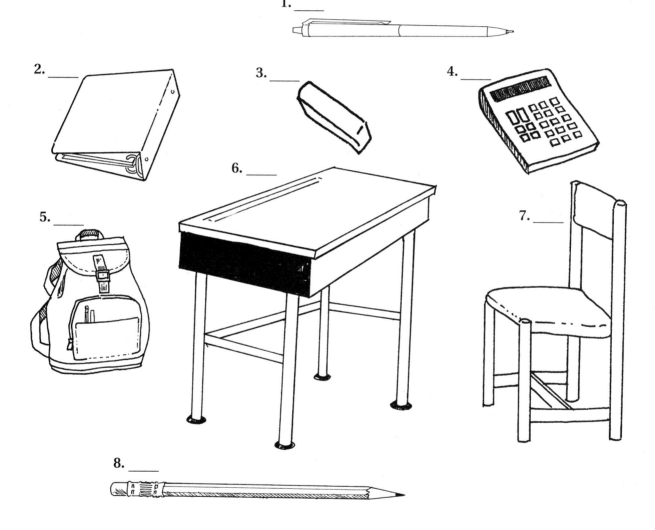

1. ____

2. ____

3. ____

4. ____

5. ____

6. ____

7. ____

8. ____

**B** Match the things that you usually use together.

1. una matita e ____

2. un foglio di carta e ____

3. un tavolo e ____

    **a.** una sedia

    **b.** una penna

    **c.** una gomma

*Invitation to Languages*

**C** Underline the appropriate expression to be used when you receive a present or a favor from someone.

  1. Grazie.
  2. Come stai?

**D** Write the missing letter of each word.

  1. una ma____ita

  2. una penn____

  3. un ta____olo

  4. un libr____

  5. una ca____colatrice

  6. uno zain____

Now put the missing letters together to form a word. _____

**E** Circle the two expressions that mean the same thing in Italian.
  1. Cosa è?
  2. Come sta?
  3. Che cos'è?

*In classe* 75

WELCOME TO ITALIAN

# 4 Numeri

**A** Write the number.

1. tre _____         5. trecento _____

2. tredici _____     6. trecentotrentatrè _____

3. trenta _____      7. tremilatrecentotrentatrè _____

4. trentatrè _____

**B** Write the number.

1. otto _____        6. cinquanta _____

2. diciotto _____    7. nove _____

3. ottanta _____     8. diciannove _____

4. cinque _____      9. novanta _____

5. quindici _____

**C** Write the following famous years in American history.

1. millequattrocentonovantadue _____

2. millesettecentosettantasei _____

**D** Match the historical event with the year indicated above.

1. _____ l'indipendenza degli Stati Uniti

2. _____ Cristoforo Colombo ha scoperto l'America.

**A** Put the expressions in the order in which they would be used.

1. ____ **a.** Prego.     2. ____ **a.** Per piacere.

____ **b.** Grazie.        ____ **b.** Grazie.

____ **c.** Per favore.    ____ **c.** Prego.

**B** Circle the letter of the expression that means the same thing.

| **1.** Ciao! | **2.** Per favore. | **3.** Arrivederci! |
|---|---|---|
| **a.** Buona sera! | **a.** Grazie. | **a.** Ci vediamo! |
| **b.** Buon giorno! | **b.** Prego. | **b.** Buon giorno! |
| **c.** Come stai? | **c.** Per piacere. | **c.** A domani! |

**C** Look at the following list of foods. Indicate if each is something to eat, *Per mangiare* or to drink, *Per bere.*

|  | *Per mangiare* | *Per bere* |
|---|---|---|
| **1.** una limonata | _____ | _____ |
| **2.** un' insalata verde | _____ | _____ |
| **3.** un'aranciata | _____ | _____ |
| **4.** pasta | _____ | _____ |
| **5.** un caffè espresso | _____ | _____ |
| **6.** spinaci | _____ | _____ |
| **7.** un tè | _____ | _____ |
| **8.** una patata | _____ | _____ |
| **9.** un cappuccino | _____ | _____ |
| **10.** una bistecca | _____ | _____ |

WELCOME TO ITALIAN

**D** Look at this menu in an Italian restaurant. Work with a classmate. Each of you will tell what you are going to order. If you aren't sure what something is, find out from someone in the class. For example, you can ask: *Che cos'è* _____ ? and find out if someone else can help.

## La Trattoria Venezia

| | |
|---|---|
| Antipasto misto | L 7,000 |
| Insalata | L 6,000 |
| Minestrone | L 8,000 |
| Prosciutto e melone | L 8,500 |
| Fettucine | L 9,000 |
| Lasagne | L 8,000 |
| Ravioli | L 8,500 |
| Tortellini | L 9,000 |
| Spaghetti | L 7,000 |
| Gnocchi | L 7,500 |
| Salmone | L 10,000 |
| Calamari | L 12,000 |
| Cappone | L 9,000 |
| Bistecca alla griglia | L 10,500 |
| Frutta fresca | L 4,000 |

 **Che ora è?**

**A** **Match the time with each clock.**

**a.** Sono le otto e mezzo.        **b.** Sono le dieci e venticinque.
**c.** È l'una e un quarto.         **d.** Sono le due e quarantacinque.
**e.** Sono le sei.                 **f.** Sono le due e dieci.

1. ____     2. ____     3. ____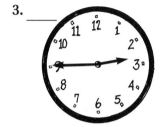

4. ____ 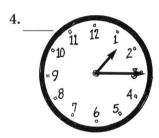    5. ____ 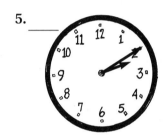    6. ____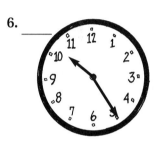

**B** **Match the expressions that mean the same thing.**

**1.** ____ Sono le cinque e trenta.        **a.** Sono le cinque e un quarto.

**2.** ____ Sono le cinque e quindici.      **b.** Sono le sei meno venti.

**3.** ____ Sono le cinque e quaranta.      **c.** Sono le cinque e mezzo.

 # I *giorni della settimana*

**A** Read the following and then complete the sentence.

I giorni della settimana sono: lunedì, martedì, mercoledì, giovedì, venerdì, sabato e domenica.

Ci sono _____ giorni in una settimana.

**B** Write the name of the day according to the calendar illustrated below.

1. Che giorno è oggi? Oggi è _____.

2. E domani? _____.

| lunedì | martedì | mercoledì | giovedì | venerdì | sabato | domenica |
|--------|---------|-----------|---------|---------|--------|----------|
| 12 | 13 | 14 | 15 | 16 | 17 | 18 |

**C** Write the missing letter in each word.

1. lune____ì          2. merc____ledì          3. ____artedì

4. v____nerdì          5. lu____edì          6. g____ovedì

7. domeni____a          8. s____bato

**Now put the missing letters together to spell a day of the week in Italian.**

___ ___ ___ ___ ___ ___ ___ ___

WELCOME TO ITALIAN

# 8 *Mesi e stagioni*

**A** Complete the following statements with Arabic numbers.

1. Ci sono _____ mesi in un anno.

2. Ci sono _____ giorni in una settimana.

3. Ci sono _____ stagioni in un anno.

**B** Match the months with their season.

1. _____ i mesi dell'inverno       **a.** giugno, luglio e agosto

2. _____ i mesi della primavera   **b.** marzo, aprile e maggio

3. _____ i mesi dell'estate        **c.** dicembre, gennaio e febbraio

4. _____ i mesi dell'autunno       **d.** settembre, ottobre e novembre

**C** Complete with true information.

Il mio compleanno è il _____.

**D** Answer the following questions according to the calendar illustrated below.

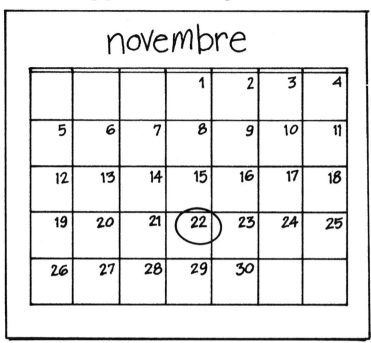

Qual è la data di oggi?

_____

**E** Complete the names of the following months with the correct letters.

1. genn_____

2. febbr_____

3. magg_____

4. g_____gno

5. lugl_____

# 9 Il tempo

**A** Write the letter of the sentence next to the illustration that goes with it.

**a.** Nevica.          **b.** Fa molto freddo.          **c.** Fa caldo.
**d.** C'è sole.          **e.** Tira vento.

1. ____
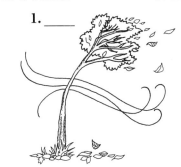

2. ____

3. ____

4. ____

5. ____

**B** Circle the letter of the most appropriate response to each question.

1. Fa bel tempo oggi?
   **a.** Sì. Piove.
   **b.** Sono le due e mezzo.
   **c.** Sì. C'è sole.

2. Che tempo fa in dicembre?
   **a.** Fa molto caldo.
   **b.** Fa freddo e nevica.
   **c.** Così, così.

3. Che tempo fa oggi?
   **a.** Bene, grazie.
   **b.** Fa brutto.
   **c.** Sono le tre e venticinque.

**C** Circle the weather expressions that mean the same thing.

1. **a.** Fa bello.
   **b.** Fa bel tempo.
   **c.** Fa brutto.

2. **a.** Fa cattivo tempo.
   **b.** Fa brutto.
   **c.** Fa bello.

WELCOME TO ITALIAN

 **10 Sono...**

**A** **Circle the letter of the appropriate response.**

1. Sei americano, Ricardo?
   a. Sì, sei americano.
   b. Sì, sono americano.
   c. Sì, è americano.

2. Sei di Chicago?
   a. No, non sono di Chicago. Sono di Denver.
   b. No, non è di Chicago. È di Denver.
   c. No, non sei di Chicago. Sei di Denver.

3. Gianni è un amico di Graziana?
   a. Sì, sono un amico di Graziana.
   b. Sì, è un amico di Graziana.
   c. Sì, sei un amico di Graziana.

**B** **Complete the following conversations with *sei, sono,* or *è*.**

—Anna Maria, _____ un'amica di Gianni Lombardi?

—Sì, io _____ un'amica di Gianni.

—_____ francese Gianni?

—No, non _____ francese. _____ italiano.

—Anche tu _____ italiana, non è vero?

—Sì, _____ italiana.

**C** **Complete the following with *-o* or *-a*.**

Anna Maria è un'amic____ molto buon____. Anna Maria non è

american____. È italian____. E Marco è un amic____ molto buon____.

Marco non è italian____. Marco è american____.

# 11 *Parlo italiano*

**A** Complete each dialogue by adding the correct endings. Then work with a classmate to ask and answer the questions together.

1. —Tu parl____ russo?

   —Io? No! Non parl____ russo.

   —No?

   —Io, no. Ma Svetlana parla russo.

2. —Parl____ inglese?

   —Chi? Io?

   —Sì, tu.

   —Sì, parl____ inglese. Parl____ anche italiano.

**B** Find the names of languages in the following puzzle. Circle each language you find. The name can be read from left to right, right to left, top to bottom, bottom to top, or diagonally.

```
C I N O L T E P R L R
I T F T I E S O O U R
E A R R N S E T I T A
S L A R A E N S N R B
E I N N E N O O G I Q
N A C I O C C A L O P
O N A G L R S E E L O
P O R T O G H E S E L
P L A N P I O R E E A
A A B O S A P P O L C
I C O C E R G I A N C
G I O L O N G A P S O
```

*Parlo italiano*  **85**

WELCOME TO ITALIAN

When you have completed the puzzle, use the bold letters to form a word. The letters spell the name of a person:

____ ____ ____ ____ ____

Then change one letter in the name to make a new word.

____ ____ ____ ____ ____

Use the new words in a sentence.

_____

_____ .

**C** Note that many words that start with a capital letter in English do not have a capital letter in Italian.

Days: lunedì, martedì
Months: gennaio, febbraio
Languages: italiano, francese

**Complete the following sentences with the appropriate letter.**

1. Oggi è ____enerdì.

2. È il primo di ____uglio.

3. Parlo ____nglese e ____taliano.

WELCOME TO ITALIAN

# Welcome to
# LATIN!

# Salvē et Valē

**A** **Choose the correct response.**

1. If you had to greet someone in front of the *Forum Rōmānum* during the time of the Romans, what would you say?
   **a.** Valē.          **b.** Salvē.

2. How would you say "good-bye" to someone?
   **a.** Valē.          **b.** Salvē.

**B** **Complete the following dialogue.**

# ②·Numerī

**A** Give the correct numbers using Arabic numerals.

1. ūnus _____      5. octō _____

2. ūndecim _____   6 centum _____

3. sex _____       7. vīgintī _____

4. duo _____       8. mille _____

**B** Match each Roman numeral with its Arabic equivalent.

**a.** 22     **c.** 10     **e.** 20     **g.** 1010
**b.** 660     **d.** 110     **f.** 18     **h.** 66

1. ____ X          4. ____ XX          7. ____ XXII

2. _____ XVIII     5. ____ CX          8. ____ MX

3. ____ LXVI       6. ____ DCLX

**C** Use Arabic numbers to write the Roman numerals found on this crypt.

_____

WELCOME TO LATIN

**D** **Choose the correct word to complete each statement.**

| | | |
|---|---|---|
| unison | quadriplegic | decimal |
| unite | century | duet |
| triplicate | quarters | octet |
| trio | octave | sextet |

1. A _____ is a group of three.

2. A _____ is a period of one hundred years.

3. The two of them sang a lovely _____.

4. All must come together as one and _____ for the same cause.

5. The whole can be divided into four _____.

6. When doing math, don't forget to put the _____ point

   in the correct place.

7. The musical scale has eight notes. Eight notes make up an

   _____.

8. An _____ is a group of eight. Eight singers, for example, form

   an _____ and six singers form a _____.

9. A _____ is a person who has lost the use of all four limbs—both

   legs and both arms.

10. All those in favor yelled in _____.

11. I need three copies, so please prepare this in _____.

# 3 Paulus et Clāra

**A** Indicate whether the following words refer to a male or a female.

|  | male | female |  | male | female |
|---|---|---|---|---|---|
| 1. Claudia | ___ | ___ | 2. Fabius | ___ | ___ |
| 3. amīcus | ___ | ___ | 4. discipula | ___ | ___ |
| 5. amīca | ___ | ___ | 6. alumnus | ___ | ___ |
| 7. discipulus | ___ | ___ | 8. alumna | ___ | ___ |
| 9. Rōmānus | ___ | ___ | 10. Rōmāna | ___ | ___ |

**B** Complete these sentences with *-a* or *-us.*

1. Paulus discipul____ bon____ est.

2. Flavia discipul____ bon____ est.

3. Flavia est quoque amīc____ bon____.

4. Paulus est Rōmān____ et Flavia quoque Rōmān____ est.

**C** Change these statements to questions.

1. Est Paulus Rōmānus. _____

2. Paulus est discipulus Rōmānus. _____

3. Rōmāna Claudia est. _____

4. Est Claudia amīca bona. _____

**D** Match the opposites.

1. ___ magnus    **a.** valē

2. ___ bonus    **b.** malus

3. ___ salvē    **c.** parvus

WELCOME TO LATIN

© Copyright Glencoe/McGraw-Hill    *Paulus et Clāra*    **91**

# 4 Amīcī et Discipulī

**A** Complete the following sentences with the appropriate letter.

1. Fabius et Caesar sunt amīc____.

2. Sunt amīc____ bon____.

3. Fabius et Caesar sunt quoque discipul____.

4. Sunt discipul____ bon____.

5. Claudia et Anna sunt amīc____.

6. Claudia et Anna sunt puell____.

7. Puell____ bon____ amīc____ sunt.

8. Claudia et Anna sunt quoque discipul____ bon____.

**B** Write the plural forms of the following words.

1. amīca bona _____

2. discipulus bonus _____

3. casa parva _____

4. villa magna _____

5. amīcus Rōmānus _____

6. alumnus et alumna _____

© Copyright Glencoe/McGraw-Hill

**C** Write the following sentences in the plural. Make all the necessary changes.

1. Paula est puella.

Paula et Claudia _____.

2. Claudia est amīca bona.

Paula et Claudia _____.

3. Cornēlius est discipulus Rōmānus.

Cornēlius et Augustus _____.

4. Cornēlius est discipulus bonus.

Cornēlius et Augustus _____.

**D** Choose the correct question word, *Quis, Qui,* or *Quae* to complete each question.

1. _____ est amīcus bonus?
Augustus est amīcus bonus.

2. _____ est discipula bona?
Minerva discipula bona est.

3. _____ sunt discipulī?
Caesar et Marcus sunt discipulī.

4. _____ sunt puellae Rōmānae?
Anna et Flavia sunt puellae Rōmānae.

**E** Identify the following.

1. paenīnsula
2. īnsula
3. īnsula parva
4. paenīnsula magna

a. ____

b. ____

c. ____

d. ____

*Amīcī et Discipulī*    **93**

WELCOME TO LATIN

# 5 *Amīcus amīcam videt*

**A** Make three sentences in Latin. Use the same words but change the word order each time.

1. Paulus / videt / Minervam

   a. _____

   b. _____

   c. _____

2. Jūlia / amat / Marcum

   a. _____

   b. _____

   c. _____

**B** Choose the correct completion.

1. Paulus _____ videt.
   a. Flavia
   b. Flaviam

2. Minerva _____ videt.
   a. Cornēlius
   b. Cornēlium

3. Minerva _____ amat.
   a. Cornēlius
   b. Cornēlium

4. Et Cornēlius _____ amat.
   a. Minerva
   b. Minervam

5. Cornēlius _____ scrībit.
   a. epistula
   b. epistulam

**C** Complete the following sentences with the correct endings.

1. Paulus, discipul_____ Rōmān_____, epistul_____ scrībit.

2. Livia, discipul_____ Rōmān_____, epistul_____ legit.

3. Paul_____ Livi_____ amat.

4. Paul_____ bon_____ amīc_____ Livi_____ amat.

5. Livi_____ Paul_____ amat.

6. Livi_____ bon_____ amīc_____ Paul_____ amat.

D. Choose the correct question word, *Quis* or *Quem* to complete each statement.

1. _____ est discipulus Rōmānus?

2. _____ amat discipulus Rōmānus?

3. _____ amat discipula Rōmāna?

*Amícus amícam videt*

# **A** **M**ottos in Latin

**A** Even today, Latin is used in many sayings and mottos. Here are some of the famous ones.

**Veni, vidi, vici.** I came, I saw, I conquered.
*Uttered by Caesar after a short, brilliant military campaign.*

**Ne cede malis.** Do not yield to misfortunes.
*A quote from Virgil, the greatest Latin epic poet.*

**cum grano salis** with a grain of salt
*A quote from Pliny the Elder, famous Roman writer and military leader.*

**Carpe diem.** Seize the day.
*From the famous Roman lyric poet, Ovid.*

**Parvum parva decent.** Small things become the small.
*From Horace, the greatest of Rome's lyric poets.*

**Amicus est alter idem.** A friend is a second self.
*From Cicero's famous Essay on Friendship.*

**Accipere quem facere iniuriam praestat.**
It is better to suffer a wrong than to do one.
*A quote from Cicero, Rome's greatest orator and person of letters.*

**Semper fidelis.** Always faithful.
*From the United States Marines.*

*State mottos:*

| | |
|---|---|
| North Carolina | **Melius esse quam videri.** Better to be than to seem. |
| South Carolina | **Dum spiro, spero.** While I breathe, I hope. |
| Arizona | **Deus ditat.** God enriches. |
| Colorado | **Nil sine numine.** Nothing without divine guidance. |
| Michigan | **Si quaeris peninsulam amoenam, circumspice.** If you are seeking a charming peninsula, look about you. |
| Washington, D.C. | **Iustitia omnibus.** Justice to all. |
| Oklahoma | **Labor omnia vincit.** Work conquers all. |

**B** Find out if your state's motto is in Latin. Chances are it is. What is the motto in Latin and what does it mean in English?

_____

_____

# Welcome to
# GERMAN!

# 1 Begrüßung

**A** Choose the correct completions to this conversation.

1. **a.** Wie geht es Ihnen?
   **b.** Wie geht's?
2. **a.** dir
   **b.** mir
3. **a.** gut
   **b.** schlecht

Tag, Hans.

Tag, Ingrid. ___

Es geht. Und ___?

Nicht ___, danke.

**B** In each of the following, circle the expression that is the more formal.

1. **a.** Tag.           **b.** Guten Tag.
2. **a.** Wie geht's?     **b.** Wie geht es Ihnen?
3. **a.** Und Ihnen?      **b.** Und dir?

**C** Match the conversation with the picture.

1. —Tag, Erika.
   —Tag, Dieter. Wie geht's?       ___
   —Es geht. Und dir?
   —Nicht schlecht, danke.

2. —Guten Tag, Frau Müller.         ___
       Wie geht es Ihnen?
   —Es geht mir sehr gut, danke.
       Und Ihnen?
   —Sehr gut, danke.

NAME _____ DATE _____

# *Verabschieden*

**A** Circle all the possible responses you would use in taking leave of someone.

1. Wie geht's?    2. Tschüß.    3. Bis bald.
4. Sehr gut.    5. Bis morgen.    6. Danke.
7. Auf Wiedersehen.

**B** Choose the expression you would use in each of the following situations.

a. Auf Wiedersehen.    b. Bis später.    c. Bis gleich.
d. Bis morgen.    e. Tschüß.

1. ____ You're saying "good-bye" to a friend whom you expect to see again soon.

2. ____ You're saying "bye" to an older person who is leaving on a trip.

3. ____ You're saying "so long" to a close friend.

4. ____ You're saying "good-bye" to someone you expect to see again tomorrow.

5. ____ You're saying "bye" to someone you expect to see again fairly soon.

**C** Match the following conversations with the pictures.

1. —Tschüß, Ingrid.
   —Tschau, Erik. Bis morgen.

2. —Wie geht's?
   —Sehr gut, danke. Und dir?
   —Gut auch.

a. ____                           b. ____

WELCOME TO GERMAN

© Copyright Glencoe/McGraw-Hill                    *Verabschieden*    **99**

# Im Klassenzimmer

**A** Match the word with the illustration.

    **a.** ein Buch     **b.** ein Kugelschreiber     **c.** ein Tisch

    **d.** ein Rucksack     **e.** eine Kreide     **f.** ein Rechner

    **g.** ein Bleistift     **h.** ein Schwamm

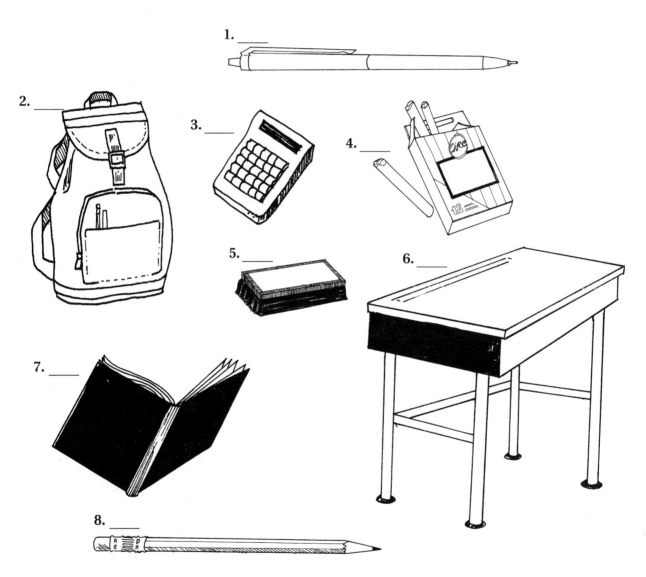

1. _____

2. _____

3. _____

4. _____

5. _____

6. _____

7. _____

8. _____

**B** Match the things that you usually use together.

a. Schwamm          c. Bleistift
b. Tisch            d. Kugelschreiber

1. der ____ und der Stuhl

2. die Kreide und der ____

3. ein Stück Papier und der ____ oder der ____

**C** Write the missing letter.

1. der K____gelschreiber

2. der F____ller

3. der ____lock

4. der St____hl

5. der Rechne____

6. die Krei____e

**D** Note that unlike English, all German nouns begin with a capital letter. Complete the following.

1. der ____ucksack

2. der ____isch

3. ein ____tück ____apier

4. das ____uch

5. der ____leistift

*Im Klassenzimmer*          **101**

WELCOME TO GERMAN

# 4 Die Zahlen

**A** Write the number.

1. eins      _____

2. elf      _____

3. einundzwanzig      _____

4. (ein)hundert      _____

5. drei      _____

6. dreizehn      _____

7. dreißig      _____

8. dreiunddreißig      _____

9. dreihundertdreiunddreißig      _____

10. dreitausend      _____

**B** Write the number.

1. zwölf      _____

2. fünfzehn      _____

3. achtzig      _____

4. fünfundsechzig      _____

5. achtundneunzig      _____

**C** Jot down the following telephone numbers.

Wie ist die Telefonnummer, bitte?

1. neun-drei-drei-fünf-vier-acht _____

2. dreiundneunzig-fünfunddreißig-achtundvierzig _____

3. zwölf-zweiundzwanzig-sechzig _____

4. fünfundachtzig-vierundsiebzig-dreizehn _____

# Umgangsformen

**A** **Match the expression(s) with the illustration.**

**1.** Eine Tasse Kaffee, bitte.

**2. a.** Danke sehr.
**b.** Bitte schön.

**3. a.** Bitte.
**b.** Danke.

**B** **Look at this menu in a German restaurant. Work with a classmate. Each of you will tell what you are going to order. If you aren't sure what something is, find out from someone in the class. For example, you can ask:** *Was ist das?* **and find out if someone else can help.**

**Matterhorn**

| | |
|---|---|
| Salat | DM 4,95 |
| Heringsalat | DM 6,50 |
| Suppe | DM 2,60 |
| Bratwurst | DM 3,50 |
| Wienerschnitzel | DM 9,60 |
| Sauerbraten mit Kartoffelkloß | DM 12,50 |
| Apfelstrudel | DM 3,50 |
| Pudding | DM 3,20 |
| Karamelpudding | DM 3,50 |
| Vanilleeis | DM ,85 |

**C** **Look at the names of the following foods in German. Can you guess what they are?**

**1.** der Sellerie _____

**2.** der Broccoli _____

**3.** der Apfel _____

**4.** die Wassermelone _____

**5.** das Filet Mignon _____

**6.** die Salami _____

**7.** die Tomate _____

**8.** die Thunfisch _____

# 6 **D**ie *Uhrzeit*

**A** Match the time with each clock.

a. Es ist elf Uhr fünf.    b. Es ist zwei Uhr zehn.
c. Es ist zehn Uhr.    d. Es ist sechs Uhr fünfundzwanzig.
e. Es ist halb neun.    f. Es ist vier Uhr vierzig.

1. ____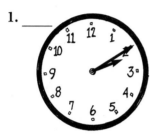

2. ____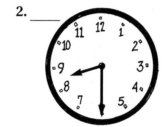

3. ____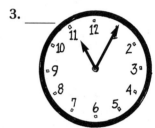

4. ____

5. ____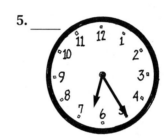

6. ____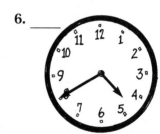

# Die Tage

**A** Note that the days of the week in German are capitalized the same as they are in English. Complete the following with the missing letters.

1. ____ontag

2. ____ienstag

3. ____ittwoch

4. ____onnerstag

5. ____reitag

6. ____amstag

7. ____onntag

**B** Answer based on the calendar.

| Montag | Dienstag | Mittwoch | Donnerstag | Freitag | Samstag | Sonntag |
|--------|----------|----------|------------|---------|---------|---------|
| 28 | 29 | 30 | 1 | 2 | 3 | 4 |
|  |  |  |  |  |  |  |

1. Welcher Tag ist heute? _____

2. Und welcher Tag ist morgen? _____

**C** Explain in your own words why Wednesday is called *Mittwoch.*

_____

_____

_____

WELCOME TO GERMAN

# **D**ie Monate und die Jahreszeiten

**A** Write the missing letter to give the name of a month.

1. O____tober

2. De____ember

3. ____uli

4. Ma____

5. M____rz

**B** Some months in German are exactly the same as in English. Which ones are they?

_____

_____

_____

_____ `

**C** Complete the following statements.

1. Es gibt _____ Monate in einem Jahr.

2. Es gibt _____ Tage in einer Woche.

3. Es gibt _____ Jahreszeiten in einem Jahr.

**D** Choose the correct months.

1. ____ das Winter      **a.** März, April und Mai

2. ____ der Frühling    **b.** Dezember, Januar und Februar

3. ____ der Sommer      **c.** September, Oktober und November

4. ____ der Herbst      **d.** Juni, Juli und August

**E** Complete the following sentences.

1. Der _____ hat achtundzwanzig Tage.

2. Der _____, der _____, der _____, und

   der_____ haben dreißig Tage.

3. Der _____, der _____, der _____, der _____,

   der _____, der _____, und der _____ haben
   einunddreißig Tage.

WELCOME TO GERMAN

# 9 Das Wetter

**A** Write the letter of the sentence next to the picture it describes.

a. Es ist windig.  b. Es schneit.  c. Es ist sonnig.
d. Es regnet.  e. Es ist so warm.  f. Es ist sehr kalt.

1. _____

2. _____

3. _____

4. _____

5. _____

6. _____

WELCOME TO GERMAN

**B** Indicate if these statements are *richtig* (R) or *falsch* (F).

1. ____ Es schneit im Winter.

2. ____ Es ist immer sehr sonnig im April.

3. ____ Es regnet im April.

4. ____ Es ist sehr warm im Dezember.

5. ____ Es ist nicht zu warm. Es ist nicht zu kalt. Es ist kühl.

**C** Circle the expressions that describe the topic sentence correctly. There may be more than one correct answer.

1. Das Wetter ist schön.
   a. Es ist sonnig.
   b. Es ist bewölkt.
   c. Es regnet.
   d. Es ist warm.
   e. Es ist schön.

2. Es ist schlecht.
   a. Es regnet.
   b. Es ist sonnig.
   c. Das Wetter ist nicht schön.
   d. Es ist sehr kalt.
   e. Es ist schön.

WELCOME TO GERMAN

NAME _____    DATE _____

# **I**ch heiße... und ich komme aus...

**A** Choose the correct question word, *wie* or *woher,* to complete each statement in the picture.

Tag. _____ heißt du?

Und _____ kommst du, Dieter?

Ich heiße Dieter.

Ich komme aus Bremerhaven.

**B** Choose the correct completion.

1. Wie ____ du?
   a. heiße
   b. heißt

2. Ich ____ Erika.
   a. heiße
   b. heißt

3. Woher ____ du, Erika?
   a. komme
   b. kommst

4. Ich ____ aus Stuttgart.
   a. komme
   b. kommst

5. Woher ____ Sie, Herr Brecht?
   a. kommst
   b. kommen

**C** Answer the following personal questions.

1. Wie heißt du? _____

2. Woher kommst du? _____

© Copyright Glencoe/McGraw-Hill

WELCOME TO GERMAN

**D** See how much German you know. Match each picture with the
correct sentence.

**a.** Er singt.　　　**b.** Sie schwimmt.　　　**c.** Sie studiert und lernt.

1. ____　　　　　　　　　　　　　　　　　2. ____

3. ____

**E** Complete the following.

1. Sing _____ du? Ja, ich singe.

2. Schwimm _____ du im Sommer? Ja, ich schwimme im Sommer.

3. Studier _____ du viel? Ja, ich studiere viel.

4. Lern _____ du? Ja, ich lern _____.

# Reading in German

**A** Read the following story about Werner and Barbara. You will be amazed how easy it is to read in German.

Werner ist ein Freund von Barbara und Barbara ist eine Freundin von Werner. Werner ist fünfzehn Jahre alt und er kommt aus Deutschland. Er kommt aus München. Natürlich spricht Werner Deutsch. Er spricht auch English, aber er spricht nicht so gut. Er spricht nur ein bißchen Englisch.

Barbara kommt nicht aus Deutschland. Sie kommt aus den USA, aus Amerika. Barbara ist auch fünfzehn Jahre alt. Barbara spricht Englisch und Deutsch. Sie spricht sehr gut Deutsch. Sie spricht immer Deutsch mit Werner.

**B** It is sometimes necessary to guess at the meaning of a new word when reading. You can very often get the meaning of a new word from the way the word is used in the sentence. This is called getting "meaning from context." From the context of these sentences, guess at the meaning of the word *spricht*.

Werner kommt aus Deutschland. Werner spricht Deutsch.
Barbara kommt aus den USA. Barbara spricht Englisch.

*Spricht* means _____.

**C** Answer the following questions.

1. Wer ist ein Freund von Barbara? _____

2. Wer ist eine Freundin von Werner? _____

3. Wer kommt aus Deutschland? _____

4. Wer kommt aus den USA? _____

5. Wer spricht ein bißchen Englisch? _____

6. Wer spricht Englisch und Deutsch? _____

7. Woher kommt Werner? _____

8. Woher kommt Barbara? _____

# Welcome to
# Japanese!

# Jiko shookai

**A** **Select the correct response. Circle the corresponding letter.**

1. What do you say in Japanese to a person you have just been introduced to?
   **a.** Sumimasen.
   **b.** Doozo yoroshiku.
   **c.** Soo desu.

2. What would you say if you wanted to excuse yourself to get someone's attention because you want to speak?
   **a.** Sumimasen.
   **b.** Doozo yoroshiku.
   **c.** Hajimemashite.

3. How would you ask someone if he/she is the person you think he/she is?
   **a.** Hanada desu.
   **b.** Hai, soo desu.
   **c.** Hanada-san desu ka[?]

4. What would you say if you wanted to tell someone who you are?
   **a.** (name) desu.
   **b.** (name) -san desu.
   **c.** Hai, soo desu.

**B** **Select the correct answer.**

1. When do you use the title *-san* in Japanese?
   **a.** When speaking about myself and using my own name.
   **b.** When using another person's name.

**C** **Choose the correct missing words to complete the following conversation.**

**a.** desu          **b.** ka          **c.** soo          **d.** doozo

—Hanada-san desu ____[?]

—Hai, ____ desu.

—Buraun ____. Hajimemashite. ____ yoroshiku.

# 2 *Go-aisatsu*

**A** Select the appropriate greeting for the time of the day.

   **a.** Ohayoo gozaimasu.    **b.** Konnichi wa.    **c.** Konban wa.

1. ____    2. ____

3. ____

**B** Indicate whether or not the following mini-conversations make sense.

|  | Yes | No |
|---|---|---|
| **1.** —Konnichi wa.<br>—Konnichi wa. | ____ | ____ |
| **2.** —Ohayoo gozaimasu.<br>—Konban wa. | ____ | ____ |
| **3.** —O-genki desu ka?<br>—Ee, genki desu. | ____ | ____ |

**C** Circle possible responses to the question: *O-genki desu ka[?]*

   **a.** Okagesama de, genki desu.
   **b.** Konnichi wa.
   **c.** Genki desu.
   **d.** Hai, arigatoo gozaimasu.
   **e.** Sumimasen.

*Go-aisatsu*    **115**

WELCOME TO JAPANESE

**D** **Select the correct answer and circle the corresponding letter.**

1. Instead of saying *O-genki desu ka[?]* to a person you have seen recently, what would you more commonly say?
   **a.** Sumimasen.
   **b.** Ii o-tenki desu ne[?]
   **c.** Okagesama de, genki desu.

2. How would you respond to the question *Ii o-tenki desu ne[?]*
   **a.** Genki desu.
   **b.** Hajimemashite.
   **c.** Ee, soo desu ne.

**E** **Select what you would say.**
   **a.** ne          **b.** ne(e)

1. ____ You agree with what a person has just said to you.

2. ____ You want to find out if the person you're speaking to agrees with you.

**F** *Desu* **is a frequently used word in Japanese. Complete the following with *desu*. Then practice these short conversations with a classmate.**

1. —Sumimasen. Hanada-san _____ ka[?]

   —Hai, soo _____.

   —Buraun _____.

2. —Ii o-tenki _____ ne[?]

   —Ee, soo _____ ne.

3. —O-genki _____ ka[?]

   —Hai, arigatoo gozaimasu. Yamaguchi-san wa[?]

   —Genki _____.

# 3 Wakareru toki ni...

**A** Indicate if the following expressions are greetings or farewells.

|  | Greeting | Farewell |
|---|---|---|
| 1. Ohayoo gozaimasu. | ____ | ____ |
| 2. Shitsurei shimasu. | ____ | ____ |
| 3. Sayoonara. | ____ | ____ |
| 4. Konnichi wa. | ____ | ____ |
| 5. Dewa, mata. | ____ | ____ |

**B** Select the correct completion to each statement or question. Then practice these short conversations with a classmate.

a. Ohayoo.
b. Soo desu ne.
c. Hai, soo desu.
d. Ee, genki desu.
e. Dewa, mata.


1. —Hanada-san desu ka[?]

   _____

2. —Hanada-san, ohayoo gozaimasu.

   _____

3. —O-genki desu ka[?]

   _____

4. —Ii o-tenki desu ne[?]

   _____

5. —Shitsurei shimasu.

   _____

WELCOME TO JAPANESE

#  Kyooshitsu

**A** Match the illustration with the word.

   **a.** hon         **b.** kaban        **c.** chooku

   **d.** keisanki    **e.** booru-pen   **f.** nooto

   **g.** enpitsu     **h.** konpyuutaa

1. ____

2. ____

3. ____

4. ____

5. ____

6. ____

7. ____

8. ____

WELCOME TO JAPANESE

#  5 *Suu-ji*

**A** Give the correct numeral.

1. ichi _____        7. go-juu-go _____

2. juu-ichi _____        8. hachi _____

3. ni-juu-ichi _____        9. juu-hachi _____

4. go _____        10. hachi-juu _____

5. juu-go _____        11. hachi-juu-hachi _____

6. go-juu _____

**B** Write the numbers in Japanese using Roman (English) letters.

1. 1 _____        6. 26 _____

2. 5 _____        7. 8 _____

3. 10 _____        8. 88 _____

4. 4 _____        9. 100 _____

5. 50 _____        10. 79 _____

**C** Add up the numbers on the dominos and write them using Roman (English) letters.

1. _____

2. _____

3. _____

4. _____

5. _____

6. _____

7. _____

8. _____

*Suu-ji*   **119**

# 6 Jikan

**A** Match the correct time with the clock. Write the correct letter in the space provided.

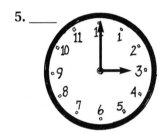

1. ____

2. ____

3. ____

4. ____

5. ____

**a.** —Nan-ji desu ka[?]
—Ni-ji han desu.

**b.** —Nan-ji desu ka[?]
—Roku-ji desu.

**c.** —Nan-ji desu ka[?]
—Juu-ichi-ji han desu.

**d.** —Nan-ji desu ka[?]
—San-ji desu.

**e.** —Nan-ji desu ka[?]
—Ku-ji han desu.

# 7 Resutoran de...

**A** Match the word with the illustration.

**a.** supagetti      **b.** piza      **c.** sarada
**d.** juusu      **e.** hanbaagaa      **f.** omuretsu

1. ____
2. ____
3. ____
4. ____
5. ____
6. ____

WELCOME TO JAPANESE

**B** Order the following items. Use the polite expression *o onegai–shimasu.*

1. hanbaagaa

_____

2. onion ringu

_____

3. hanbaagaa to onion ringu

_____

4. sarada

_____

**C** Choose the correct expression to complete the following mini-conversations. Then practice them with a classmate.

a. arimasu          b. to              c. Sumimasen
d. desu             e. hai             f. gozaimasu
g. ka               h. onegai-shimasu  i. ikura

1. ____. Chiizu baagaa wa arimasu ____[?]

   Hai, ____.

   Chiizu baagaa o ____.

2. ____. Hanbaagaa wa ____ ka[?]

   ____, arimasu.

   ____ desu ka[?]

   200-en desu.

3. Hanbaagaa ____ orenji juusu o ____.

   Arigatoo ____. Ikura desu ka[?]

   450-en ____.

**D** Indicate if the following Japanese dishes are meat or fish dishes.

|                | Meat | Fish |
|----------------|------|------|
| 1. sushi       | ____ | ____ |
| 2. sukiyaki    | ____ | ____ |
| 3. shabu shabu | ____ | ____ |
| 4. tempura     | ____ | ____ |

# Nani-go o hanashimasu ka[?]

**A** Select the appropriate word to complete each sentence.

**a. Iie**      **b. Hai**      **c. sukoshi**

**1.** Hanashimasu ka[?]

_____, hanashimasu.

**2.** Wakarimasu ka[?]

_____, wakarimasu.

**3.** Nihongo o hanashimasu ka[?]

_____, _____ hanashimasu.

**4.** Nihongo o hanashimasu ka[?]

_____, hanashimasen.

**B** Change the following sentences to the negative.

**1.** Nihongo o hanashimasu.

_____

**2.** Eigo ga wakarimasu.

_____

*Nani-go o hanashimasu ka[?]*      **123**

# ⑨ Nan-nichi, nan-yoobi

**A** Match the days.

1. ____ Sunday     **a.** kin'yoobi

2. ____ Friday     **b.** suiyoobi

3. ____ Monday     **c.** nichiyoobi

4. ____ Wednesday  **d.** getsuyoobi

**B** Write the numerals for the following numbers.

1. ichi      _____

2. san       _____

3. go        _____

4. shichi    _____

5. ku        _____

6. juu-ichi  _____

**C** Select which month the following holidays take place in the U.S.

1. ____ Labor Day       **a.** ichi-gatsu

2. ____ Christmas       **b.** juu-ni-gatsu

3. ____ Thanksgiving    **c.** go-gatsu

4. ____ New Year's      **d.** juu-ichi-gatsu

5. ____ Memorial Day    **e.** ku-gatsu

WELCOME TO JAPANESE

# Student Tape Manual

 **Saludos**

**A** Listen and repeat.

**B** Listen and choose.

    1. a.       b.       c.

    2. a.       b.       c.

    3. a.       b.       c.

**C** Listen and repeat.

**D** Listen and choose.

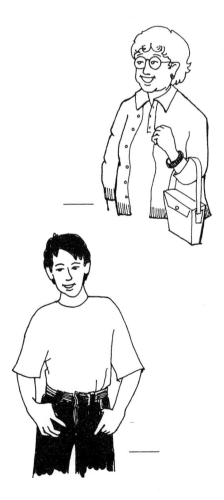

 **2 A** *diós*

**A** Listen and repeat.

**B** Listen and choose.

    1. a.      b.      c.

    2. a.      b.      c.

    3. a.      b.      c.

    4. a.      b.      c.

**C** Listen and repeat.

**D** Listen and choose.

    1. muchacha    muchacho
    2. muchacha    muchacho
    3. muchacha    muchacho
    4. muchacha    muchacho
    5. muchacha    muchacho
    6. muchacha    muchacho

WELCOME TO SPANISH

# 3 En clase

**A** Listen and repeat.

**B** Listen and choose.

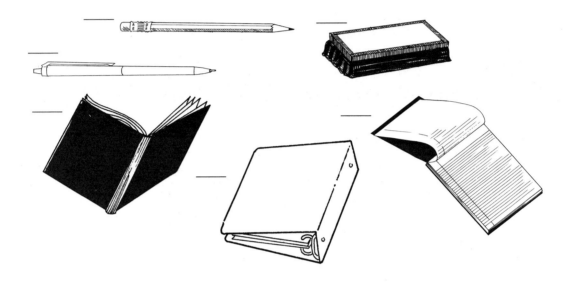

**C** Listen and ask.

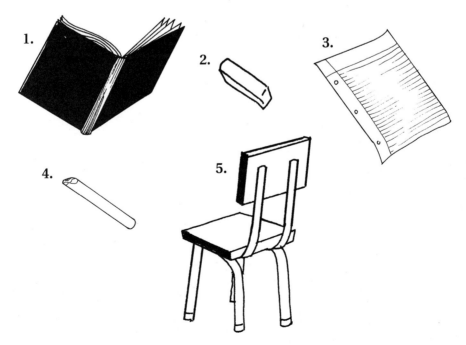

1.

2.

3.

4.

5.

 **Números**

**A** Listen and repeat.

**B** Listen and choose.

1. _____ 2. _____ 3. _____ 4. _____ 5. _____

**C** Listen and repeat.

**D** Listen and choose.

1. _____ 2. _____ 3. _____ 4. _____ 5. _____

**E** Listen and repeat.

**F** Listen and repeat.

**G** Listen and answer.

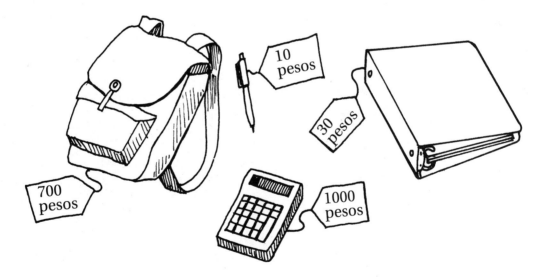

# 5 La cortesía

**A** Listen and repeat.

**B** Listen and ask.

1.

2.

3.

4.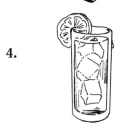

**C** Listen and answer.

 **6 L*a hora***

**A** Listen and repeat.

**B** Listen and repeat.

**C** Listen and answer.

1. _____

2. _____

3. _____

4. _____

5. _____

6. _____

1.

2.

3.

4.

5.

6.

**D** Listen and answer.

1. _____

2. _____

3. _____

4. _____

| CURSOS | HORA |
|---|---|
| Matemáticas | 8:00 |
| Español | 10:30 |
| Inglés | 2:00 |
| Ciencias | 1:15 |

# 7 Los colores

**A** Listen and repeat.

**B** Listen and answer.

1. _____

2. _____

3. _____

4. _____

# 8 Los días de la semana

**A** Listen and repeat.

**B** Listen and answer.

1. _____    2. _____

3. _____    4. _____

5. _____    6. _____

**C** Listen and choose.

1. ____    2. ____    3. ____    4. ____

5. ____    6. ____    7. ____

#  *Los meses y las estaciones*

**A** Listen and repeat.

**B** Listen and choose.

1. _____

2. _____

3. _____

4. _____

5. _____

**C** Listen and choose.

|  | 1 | 2 | 3 | 4 | 5 | 6 | 7 |
|---|---|---|---|---|---|---|---|
| el invierno |  |  |  |  |  |  |  |
| la primavera |  |  |  |  |  |  |  |
| el verano |  |  |  |  |  |  |  |
| el otoño |  |  |  |  |  |  |  |

# 10 El tiempo

**A** Listen and repeat.

**B** Listen and choose.

|  | 1 | 2 | 3 | 4 | 5 |
|---|---|---|---|---|---|
| el verano |  |  |  |  |  |
| el invierno |  |  |  |  |  |
| los dos |  |  |  |  |  |

**C** Listen and choose.

134    *Invitation to Languages*            © Copyright Glencoe/McGraw-Hill

## 11 Yo soy...

A  Listen and repeat.

B  Listen and choose.

|        | 1 | 2 | 3 | 4 | 5 | 6 |
|--------|---|---|---|---|---|---|
| verdad |   |   |   |   |   |   |
| falso  |   |   |   |   |   |   |

## 12 Soy de...

A  Listen and repeat.

B  Listen and repeat.

C  Listen and choose.

1. Sí    No        2. Sí    No

3. Sí    No        4. Sí    No

5. Sí    No        6. Sí    No

D  Listen and choose.

1. a.        b.        c.

2. a.        b.        c.

3. a.        b.        c.

WELCOME TO SPANISH

# 13 *Hablo español*

**A** Listen and repeat.

**B** Listen and react.

1. _____    2. _____

3. _____    4. _____

5. _____    6. _____

7. _____    8. _____

# 14 *Estudio...*

**A** Listen and repeat.

**B** Listen and choose.

1. a.        b.        c.            2. a.        b.        c.

3. a.        b.        c.

**C** Listen and answer.

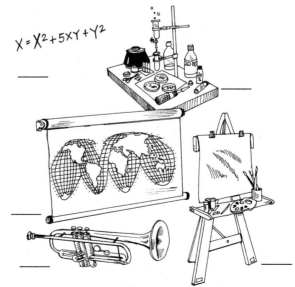

$X = X^2 + 5XY + Y^2$

# 15 Mi casa

**A** Listen and repeat.

**B** Listen and choose.

1. a.      b.      c.

2. a.      b.      c.

3. a.      b.      c.

4. a.      b.      c.

1.

2.

3.

4.

**C** Listen and answer.

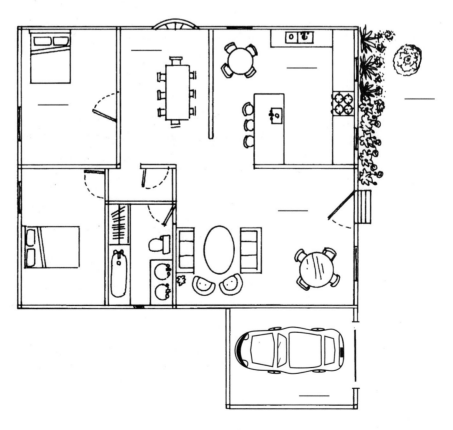

# 16 Mi familia

**A**  Listen and repeat.

**B**  Listen and answer.

|  | 1 | 2 | 3 | 4 | 5 | 6 | 7 | 8 |
|---|---|---|---|---|---|---|---|---|
| verdad | | | | | | | | |
| falso | | | | | | | | |

**C**  Listen and repeat.

*Invitation to Languages*

# 17 Mi mascota

**A** Listen and repeat.

**B** Listen and repeat.

**C** Listen and choose.

_____     _____     _____

_____     _____     _____

_____     _____

**D** Listen and choose.

1. a.     b.     c.          2. a.     b.     c.

3. a.     b.     c.          4. a.     b.     c.

5. a.     b.     c.          6. a.     b.     c.

# 18 Los deportes

**A** Listen and repeat.

**B** Listen and choose.

____

____

____

____

____

**C** Listen and choose.

    1. a.        b.

    2. a.        b.

    3. a.        b.

    4. a.        b.

    5. a.        b.

# 19 La ropa

A  **Listen and repeat.**

B  **Listen and choose.**

**L**es salutations

A Listen and repeat.

B Listen and choose.

|       | 1 | 2 | 3 | 4 |
|-------|---|---|---|---|
| vrai  |   |   |   |   |
| faux  |   |   |   |   |

C Listen and repeat.

D Listen and choose.

*Invitation to Languages*                    © Copyright Glencoe/McGraw-Hill

WELCOME TO FRENCH

#  **2** **A***u revoir*

**A**  Listen and repeat.

**B**  Listen and choose.

|  | 1 | 2 | 3 | 4 | 5 |
|---|---|---|---|---|---|
| vrai |  |  |  |  |  |
| faux |  |  |  |  |  |

**C**  Listen and repeat.

**D**  Listen and choose.

1. jeune fille      garçon
2. jeune fille      garçon
3. jeune fille      garçon
4. jeune fille      garçon
5. jeune fille      garçon
6. jeune fille      garçon

#  3 En classe

**A** Listen and repeat.

**B** Listen and choose.

1. un cahier ____
2. un stylo-bille ____
3. une gomme ____
4. un bloc ____
5. un livre ____
6. un crayon ____

**C** Listen and ask.

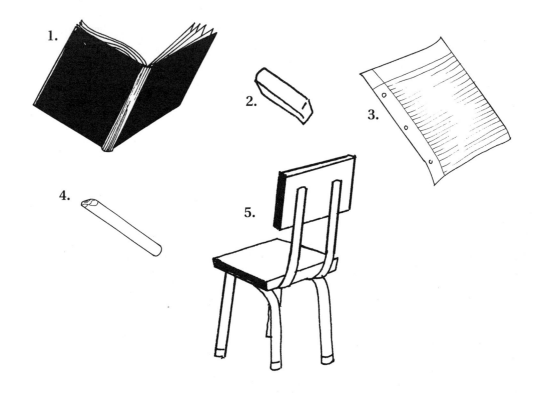

WELCOME TO FRENCH

# ❖4❖ *L es nombres*

**A** Listen and repeat.

**B** Listen and add.

1. _____  2. _____

3. _____  4. _____

5. _____

**C** Listen and repeat.

**D** Listen and circle.

| | | | | | | | | |
|---|---|---|---|---|---|---|---|---|
| 1. | 20 | 15 | 50 | 6. | 38 | 67 | 61 |
| 2. | 25 | 5 | 17 | 7. | 100 | 11 | 1 |
| 3. | 53 | 10 | 70 | 8. | 25 | 31 | 7 |
| 4. | 70 | 34 | 15 | 9. | 46 | 29 | 6 |
| 5. | 92 | 26 | 9 | 10. | 20 | 98 | 40 |

**E** Listen and repeat.

**F** Listen and repeat.

**G** Listen and answer.

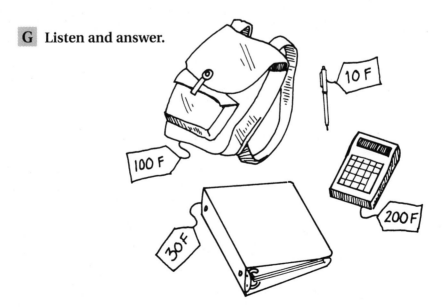

# 5 *La politesse*

**A**  Listen and repeat.

**B**  Listen and choose.

|       | 1 | 2 | 3 | 4 | 5 |
|-------|---|---|---|---|---|
| vrai  |   |   |   |   |   |
| faux  |   |   |   |   |   |

# 6 *L'heure*

**A**  Listen and repeat.

**B**  Listen and repeat.

**C**  Listen and choose.

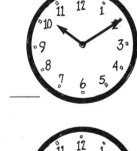    

# **7** **L**es couleurs

**A**  Listen and repeat.

**B**  Listen and answer.

1. _____
2. _____
3. _____
4. _____

# **8** **L**es jours de la semaine

**A**  Listen and repeat.

**B**  Listen and answer.

1. _____    2. _____

3. _____    4. _____

5. _____    6. _____

7. _____    8. _____

C. Listen and decide.

____ lundi        ____ mardi        ____ mercredi

____ jeudi        ____ vendredi     ____ samedi

____ dimanche

**L**es mois et les saisons

**A** Listen and repeat.

**B** Listen and choose.

|            | 1 | 2 | 3 | 4 | 5 | 6 | 7 |
|------------|---|---|---|---|---|---|---|
| printemps  |   |   |   |   |   |   |   |
| été        |   |   |   |   |   |   |   |
| automne    |   |   |   |   |   |   |   |
| hiver      |   |   |   |   |   |   |   |

**C** Listen and answer.

1. _____

2. _____

3. _____

4. _____

5. _____

6. _____

#  10 *Le temps*

**A** Listen and repeat.

**B** Listen and choose.

|            | 1 | 2 | 3 | 4 | 5 |
|------------|---|---|---|---|---|
| en été     |   |   |   |   |   |
| en hiver   |   |   |   |   |   |
| les deux   |   |   |   |   |   |

**C** Listen and choose.

_____    _____

_____    _____

_____    _____

*Student Tape Manual*   **149**

## Je suis...

**A** Listen and repeat.

**B** Listen and choose.

| | 1 | 2 | 3 | 4 | 5 |
|---|---|---|---|---|---|
| vrai | | | | | |
| faux | | | | | |

## Je suis de...

**A** Listen and repeat.

**B** Listen and repeat.

**C** Listen and choose.

1. Oui.    Non.          2. Oui.    Non.

3. Oui.    Non.          4. Oui.    Non.

5. Oui.    Non.          6. Oui.    Non.

**D** Listen and choose.

| | 1 | 2 | 3 | 4 | 5 | 6 |
|---|---|---|---|---|---|---|
| vrai | | | | | | |
| faux | | | | | | |

*Invitation to Languages* © Copyright Glencoe/McGraw-Hill

WELCOME TO FRENCH

# 13 *Je parle français*

**A** Listen and repeat.

**B** Listen and react.

1. _____

2. _____

3. _____

4. _____

5. _____

6. _____

7. _____

8. _____

#  J'aime...

**A** Listen and repeat.

**B** Listen and answer.

1. _____

2. _____

3. _____

4. _____

5. _____

**C** Listen and answer.

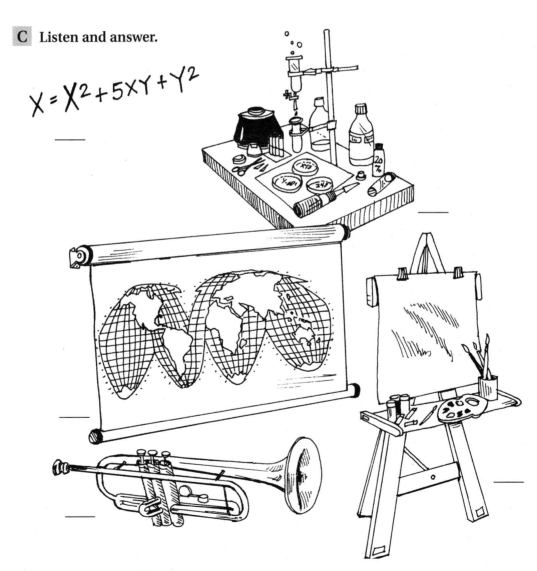

$$X = X^2 + 5XY + Y^2$$

# 15 Ma maison

**A** Listen and repeat.

**B** Listen and choose.

1. a.        b.        c.

2. a.        b.        c.

3. a.        b.        c.

4. a.        b.        c.

1.

2.

3.

**C** Listen and answer.

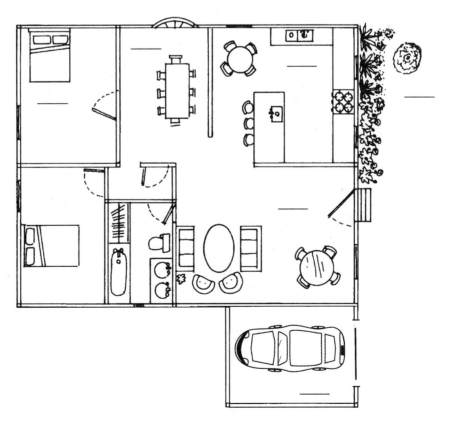

# 16 *Ma famille*

**A** Listen and repeat.

**B** Listen and choose.

Anne-Marie  Jean-Paul

Richard  Geneviève

Suzanne  Robert

Élise  Maurice

Philippe  Moi  Caroline

|       | 1 | 2 | 3 | 4 | 5 | 6 | 7 | 8 |
|-------|---|---|---|---|---|---|---|---|
| vrai  |   |   |   |   |   |   |   |   |
| faux  |   |   |   |   |   |   |   |   |

**C** Listen and repeat.

**D** Listen and repeat.

#  Un bon ami

**A**   Listen and repeat.

**B**   Listen and repeat.

**C**   Listen and choose.

  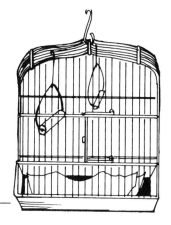  

_____     _____     _____

_____          _____     _____

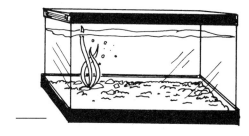  

_____               

**D**   Listen and answer.

1. _____

2. _____

3. _____

4. _____

5. _____

6. _____

*Student Tape Manual*      **155**

WELCOME TO FRENCH

# 18 L*as sports*

**A** Listen and repeat.

**B** Listen and choose.

_____

_____

_____

_____

**C** Listen and choose.

|  | 1 | 2 | 3 | 4 | 5 |
|---|---|---|---|---|---|
| soccer |  |  |  |  |  |
| tennis |  |  |  |  |  |
| both |  |  |  |  |  |
| neither |  |  |  |  |  |

# 19 Les vêtements

**A** Listen and repeat.

**B** Listen and choose.

**WELCOME TO ITALIAN**

**A** Listen and repeat.

**B** Listen and choose.

Ciao. _____        Buona sera. _____

Come sta? _____        Non c'è male. _____

Buon giorno. _____        Bene. _____

Come stai? _____        Grazie. _____

**C** Listen and repeat.

**D** Listen and choose.

|  | 1 | 2 | 3 | 4 | 5 |
|---|---|---|---|---|---|
| **vero** | | | | | |
| **falso** | | | | | |

# 2 *Arrivederci!*

**A**  Listen and repeat.

**B**  Listen and choose.

1. a.          b.          c.          2. a.          b.          c.

3. a.          b.          c.          4. a.          b.          c.

**C**  Listen and repeat.

**D**  Listen and choose.

WELCOME TO ITALIAN

#  In classe

**A** Listen and repeat.

**B** Listen and choose.

1. _____
2. _____
3. _____
4. _____
5. _____
6. _____

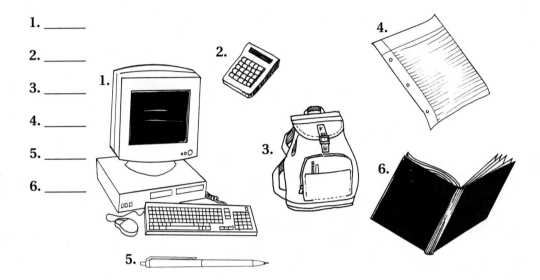

**C** Listen and choose.

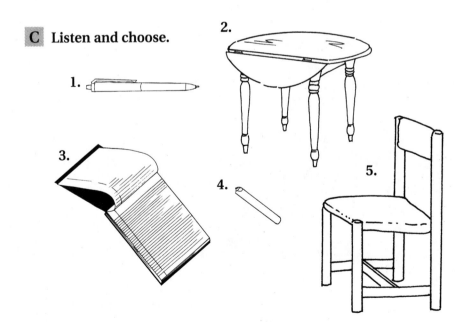

# 4 Numeri

**A** Listen and repeat.

**B** Listen and repeat.

**C** Listen and repeat.

**D** Listen and write.

1. ____   2. ____   3. ____   4. ____   5. ____

6. ____   7. ____   8. ____   9. ____   10. ____

**E** Listen and repeat.

**F** Listen and answer.

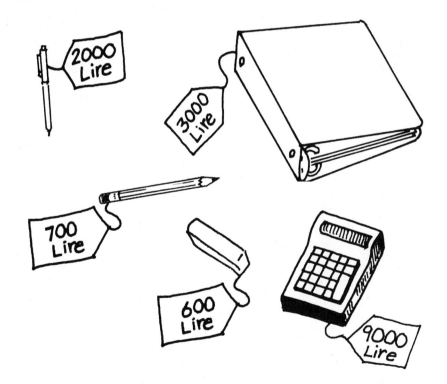

*Student Tape Manual*     **161**

WELCOME TO ITALIAN

# 5 Prego

**A** Listen and repeat.

**B** Listen and choose.

|  | 1 | 2 | 3 | 4 | 5 | 6 |
|---|---|---|---|---|---|---|
| vero |  |  |  |  |  |  |
| falso |  |  |  |  |  |  |

**C** Listen and answer.

1000 lire

2000 lire

900 lire

**Che ora è?**

**A** Listen and repeat.

**B** Listen and repeat.

**C** Listen and choose.

(P.M.)

**D** Listen and choose.

| | 1 | 2 | 3 | 4 | 5 | 6 | 7 |
|---|---|---|---|---|---|---|---|
| **vero** | | | | | | | |
| **falso** | | | | | | | |

*Student Tape Manual*   **163**

WELCOME TO ITALIAN

**I** *giorni della settimana*

**A** Listen and repeat.

**B** Listen and answer.

1. _____

2. _____

3. _____

4. _____

5. _____

6. _____

7. _____

**C** Listen and choose.

1.    Sì.        No.

2.    Sì.        No.

3.    Sì.        No.

4.    Sì.        No.

5.    Sì.        No.

WELCOME TO ITALIAN

# 8 Mesi e stagioni

**A** Listen and repeat.

**B** Listen and repeat.

**C** Listen and choose.

| | | | |
|---|---|---|---|
| primavera | _____ | giugno | _____ |
| luglio | _____ | estate | _____ |
| marzo | _____ | autunno | _____ |
| dicembre | _____ | febbraio | _____ |
| aprile | _____ | maggio | _____ |

# 9 Il tempo

**A** Listen and repeat.

**B** Listen and choose.

1. a.      b.      c.            2. a.      b.      c.

3. a.      b.      c.            4. a.      b.      c.

5. a.      b.      c.

WELCOME TO ITALIAN

*Student Tape Manual*     **165**

# 10 Sono...

**A** Listen and repeat.

**B** Listen and repeat.

**C** Listen and choose.

|         | 1 | 2 | 3 | 4 | 5 |
|---------|---|---|---|---|---|
| vero    |   |   |   |   |   |
| falso   |   |   |   |   |   |

# 11 Parlo italiano

**A** Listen and repeat.

**B** Listen and answer.

1. _____

2. _____

3. _____

4. _____

**C** Listen and choose.

|         | 1 | 2 | 3 | 4 | 5 | 6 |
|---------|---|---|---|---|---|---|
| vero    |   |   |   |   |   |   |
| falso   |   |   |   |   |   |   |

# 1  Salvē et Valē

**A**  Listen and repeat.

**B**  Listen and choose.

    1. a.      b.      c.

    2. a.      b.      c.

    3. a.      b.      c.

# 2  Numerī

**A**  Listen and repeat.

**B**  Listen and choose.

    1. ____    2. ____    3. ____    4. ____    5. ____

**C**  Listen and add.

    1. _____    2. _____

    3. _____    4. _____

    5. _____    6. _____

**D**  Listen and subtract.

    1. _____    2. _____

    3. _____    4. _____

    5. _____

WELCOME TO LATIN

## 3 Paulus et Clāra

**A** Listen and repeat.

**B** Listen and choose.

1. _____  2. _____  3. _____  4. _____

**C** Listen and react.

1. _____  2. _____

3. _____  4. _____

5. _____

## 4 Amīcī et Discipulī

**A** Listen and repeat.

**B** Listen and react.

1. _____  2. _____

3. _____  4. _____

5. _____

**C** Listen and decide.

1. _____  2. _____

3. _____  4. _____

5. _____  6. _____

WELCOME TO LATIN

# 5 Amīcus amīcam videt

**A** **Listen and repeat.**

**B** **Listen and decide.**

1. _____     2. _____

3. _____     4. _____

5. _____

**C** **Listen and decide.**

1. _____     2. _____

3. _____     4. _____

5. _____

WELCOME TO LATIN

#  Begrüßung

A Listen and repeat.

B Listen and choose.

| | 1 | 2 | 3 | 4 |
|---|---|---|---|---|
| richtig | | | | |
| falsch | | | | |

C Listen and repeat.

D Listen and choose.

| | 1 | 2 | 3 | 4 | 5 | 6 |
|---|---|---|---|---|---|---|
| formal | | | | | | |
| informal | | | | | | |

WELCOME TO GERMAN

# 2 Verabschieden

**A**  Listen and repeat.

**B**  Listen and repeat.

**C**  Listen and choose.

|          | 1 | 2 | 3 | 4 | 5 | 6 |
|----------|---|---|---|---|---|---|
| richtig  |   |   |   |   |   |   |
| falsch   |   |   |   |   |   |   |

**D**  Listen and choose.

|          | 1 | 2 | 3 | 4 | 5 |
|----------|---|---|---|---|---|
| richtig  |   |   |   |   |   |
| falsch   |   |   |   |   |   |

WELCOME TO GERMAN

# **I**m Klassenzimmer

**A** Listen and repeat.

**B** Listen and choose.

1. a.      b.      c.

2. a.      b.      c.

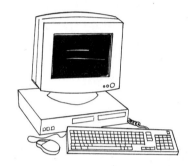

3. a.      b.      c.

**C** Listen and choose.

____ 1. der Kugelschreiber      ____ 2. der Bleistift

____ 3. der Schwamm      ____ 4. der Block

____ 5. das Buch      ____ 6. das Papier

____ 7. ein Stück Papier      ____ 8. der Computer

____ 9. der Rechner      ____ 10. der Stuhl

____ 11. der Schreibtisch      ____ 12. der Rucksack

# 4 **D**ie *Zahlen*

**A** Listen and repeat.

**B** Listen and choose.

1. _____  2. _____

3. _____  4. _____

5. _____  6. _____

**C** Listen and repeat.

**D** Listen and choose.

1. _____  2. _____

3. _____  4. _____

5. _____

**E** Listen and repeat.

**F** Listen and choose.

| | 1 | 2 | 3 | 4 |
|---|---|---|---|---|
| richtig | | | | |
| falsch | | | | |

WELCOME TO GERMAN

# Umgangsformen

**A** Listen and repeat.

**B** Listen and ask.

1.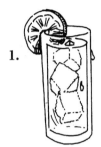

2.

3.

4.

**C** Listen and choose.

1. a.          b.          c.

2. a.          b.          c.

3. a.          b.          c.

WELCOME TO GERMAN

NAME _____  DATE _____

 **Die Uhrzeit**

**A**  Listen and repeat.

**B**  Listen and repeat.

**C**  Listen and choose.

1.     2.     3.

4.     5.     6.

WELCOME TO GERMAN

**D**  Listen and choose.

|        | 1 | 2 | 3 | 4 | 5 |
|--------|---|---|---|---|---|
| richtig |   |   |   |   |   |
| falsch  |   |   |   |   |   |

# 7 Die Tage

**A** Listen and repeat.

**B** Listen and answer.

1. _____
2. _____
3. _____
4. _____
5. _____
6. _____

**C** Listen and choose.

1. a.          b.          c.

2. a.          b.          c.

3. a.          b.          c.

# Die Monate und die Jahreszeiten

**A** Listen and repeat.

**B** Listen and choose.

|         | 1 | 2 | 3 | 4 | 5 |
|---------|---|---|---|---|---|
| richtig |   |   |   |   |   |
| falsch  |   |   |   |   |   |

**C** Listen and choose.

1. a.     b.     c.

2. a.     b.     c.

3. a.     b.     c.

4. a.     b.     c.

WELCOME TO GERMAN

# 9 Das Wetter

**A** Listen and repeat.

**B** Listen and choose.

|  | 1 | 2 | 3 | 4 | 5 |
|---|---|---|---|---|---|
| im Sommer |  |  |  |  |  |
| im Winter |  |  |  |  |  |

**C** Listen and identify.

WELCOME TO GERMAN

# Ich heiße... und ich komme aus...

**A** Listen and repeat.

**B** Listen and choose.

1. Ja.        Nein.

2. Ja.        Nein.

3. Ja.        Nein.

4. Ja.        Nein.

5. Ja.        Nein.

6. Ja.        Nein.

**C** Listen and choose.

|          | 1 | 2 | 3 | 4 | 5 | 6 |
|----------|---|---|---|---|---|---|
| richtig  |   |   |   |   |   |   |
| falsch   |   |   |   |   |   |   |

WELCOME TO GERMAN

# **J**iko shookai

**A** Listen and repeat.

**B** Listen.

**C** Listen and choose.

1. a.         b.         c.          2. a.         b.         c.

WELCOME TO JAPANESE

# 2 Go-aisatsu

**A** Listen and repeat.

**B** Listen and repeat.

**C** Listen.

**D** Listen and choose.

|  | 1 | 2 | 3 | 4 | 5 |
|---|---|---|---|---|---|
| true |  |  |  |  |  |
| false |  |  |  |  |  |

**E** Listen and match.

a.    b.    c.

1. a.      b.      c.

2. a.      b.      c.

3. a.      b.      c.

WELCOME TO JAPANESE

#  3 *W*akareru toki ni...

**A** Listen and repeat.

**B** Listen.

**C** Listen and choose.

|       | 1 | 2 | 3 | 4 | 5 |
|-------|---|---|---|---|---|
| true  |   |   |   |   |   |
| false |   |   |   |   |   |

**D** Listen and react.

1. _____

2. _____

3. _____

4. _____

5. _____

WELCOME TO JAPANESE

# 4 Kyooshitsu

**A** Listen and repeat.

**B** Listen.

**C** Listen and choose.

| | 1 | 2 | 3 | 4 | 5 |
|---|---|---|---|---|---|
| true | | | | | |
| false | | | | | |

# 5 Suu-ji

**A** Listen and repeat.

**B** Listen and choose.

1. _____     2. _____

3. _____     4. _____

5. _____

**C** Listen and repeat.

**B** Listen and choose.

1. _____     2. _____

3. _____     4. _____

5. _____

WELCOME TO JAPANESE

# 6 Jikan

**A** Listen and repeat.

**B** Listen and choose.

**C** Listen.

**D** Listen and choose.

1. a.      b.      c.           2. a.      b.      c.

# 7 Resutoran de...

**A** Listen and repeat.

**B** Listen and choose.

|          | 1 | 2 | 3 | 4 | 5 |
|----------|---|---|---|---|---|
| hungry   |   |   |   |   |   |
| thirsty  |   |   |   |   |   |

**C** Listen and repeat.

**D** Listen and choose.

1. a.        b.        c.

2. a.        b.        c.

3. a.        b.        c.

**E** Listen and choose.

|              | 1 | 2 | 3 | 4 | 5 | 6 | 7 | 8 | 9 | 10 |
|--------------|---|---|---|---|---|---|---|---|---|----|
| Nihon ryoori |   |   |   |   |   |   |   |   |   |    |
| Amerika ryoori |  |   |   |   |   |   |   |   |   |    |

WELCOME TO JAPANESE

# 8 Nani-go o hanashimasu ka[?]

**A** Listen and repeat.

**B** Listen and react.

1. _____

2. _____

3. _____

4. _____

5. _____

6. _____

7. _____

**WELCOME TO JAPANESE**

# 9 Nan-yichi, nan-yoobi

**A** Listen and repeat.

**B** Listen and answer

1. _____    2. _____

3. _____    4. _____

5. _____    6. _____

7. _____

**C** Listen and repeat.

**D** Listen and match.

| | |
|---|---|
| Yoko | hachi-gatsu |
| Noriko | ichi-gatsu |
| Michiko | ni-gatsu |
| Kiyoshi | go-gatsu |
| Haruko | juu-ni-gatsu |
| Kasumi | shi-gatsu |
| | juu-ichi-gatsu |
| | shichi-gatsu |
| | san-gatsu |
| | roko-gatsu |

WELCOME TO JAPANESE